Havin' a Ball

Havin' a Ball

My Improbable Basketball Journey

RICHIE ADUBATO

with PETER KERASOTIS

Foreword by DICK VITALE

University of Nebraska Press • LINCOLN

© 2020 by Richie Adubato and Peter Kerasotis
Foreword © 2020 by the Board of Regents of the
University of Nebraska

All rights reserved
Manufactured in the United States of America

∞

Library of Congress Cataloging-in-Publication Data
Names: Adubato, Richie, author. | Kerasotis, Peter,
author.
Title: Havin' a ball: my improbable basketball
journey / Richie Adubato, with Peter Kerasotis;
foreword by Dick Vitale.
Other titles: Having a ball
Description: Lincoln: University of Nebraska Press,
2020.
Identifiers: LCCN 2020004128
ISBN 9781496212825 (Hardback: acid-free paper)
ISBN 9781496223418 (ePub)
ISBN 9781496223425 (mobi)
ISBN 9781496223432 (PDF)
Subjects: LCSH: Basketball coaches—United
States—Biography. | Detroit Pistons (Basketball
team)—History. | Dallas Mavericks (Basketball
team)—History. | Orlando Magic (Basketball
team)—History. | New York Liberty (Basketball
team)—History. | Washington Mystics (Basketball
team)—History.
Classification: LCC GV884.A338 A3 2020 | DDC
796.323092 [B]—dc23
LC record available at
https://lccn.loc.gov/2020004128

Set in Questa by Laura Buis.

For my family—my sister, Valerie; my daughter, Beth; my sons, Scott and Adam; my grandchildren, Allegra and Sean; and most importantly, to my patient and understanding wife, Carol.—RICHIE ADUBATO

For Shelby Strother, Billy Cox, Lane Corvey, and Ben Patterson, for the kind way you nurtured what you saw in a young writer.
—PETER KERASOTIS

CONTENTS

FOREWORD

Dick Vitale

There are basketball people and then there are guys like Richie Adubato—guys who eat, drink, sleep, and breathe basketball. I'm telling you, if you're ever around Richie Adubato, it's basketball, basketball, basketball! Richie is a basketball junkie, a basketball lifer, the kind of guy I enjoy being around. And I have been around Richie Adubato most of my life.

Richie and I met when we were North Jersey high school coaches. I was the head coach at East Rutherford High School, and Richie was the head coach at Our Lady of the Valley High School in Orange. We became fast friends, and we coached at each other's camps. I was in awe of him. I still am. Richie was so impressive with his basketball knowledge, along with his ability to relate to players, to motivate and inspire people. And the stories! Oh man, Richie has a million stories! He'll have you rolling on the floor!

Back then, in the midsixties, New Jersey was a hotbed of young coaches—guys like Hubie Brown, Mike Fratello, Rollie Massimino, Lou Campanelli, and, of course, Richie. Always Richie. He was the guy always learning, always in search of knowledge. There were many nights when we would wind up at one of those Jersey diners, talking hoops, getting into verbal battles over things like how to best defend the screen and roll. That's how fanatical we were about coaching hoops.

Richie was there from the beginning, and I wanted him to be there with me when I took the University of Detroit head-coaching job in 1973. I asked him to be my assistant, but by then he had a good thing going on as the head coach at Upsala College, and he turned me down.

Five years later, when I got the Detroit Pistons' head-coaching job in 1978, I called Richie, asking him again to be my assistant. I knew he could win players over with his tremendous love for the game. I knew he had great knowledge of the game, and that he could teach it. Richie is an outstanding teacher. I've watched him do clinics, I've watched him speak, I've watched him perform on a basketball court, breaking down a game, and few can do it better than Richie Adubato. So I was thrilled that this time he accepted. It was the first time we ever coached a team together. Sadly, it was also the only time. Early in my second year there, the Pistons fired me. I think Richie was more upset than I was. It really hurt him. But that's Richie. He's loyal. And loyalty means a lot to me. Richie has been a loyal friend through thick and thin. He has that kind of loyalty you can just feel.

So it was no surprise that when the Pistons offered Richie the job after firing me, he didn't want to take it. But I told him, "Hey, go for it, man! Take the job!" He did. And while I went into broadcasting after that, where I have stayed, Richie continued on his journey of being a basketball-coaching lifer. He became an NBA head coach with the Pistons, the Dallas Mavericks, and the Orlando Magic; an assistant with the New York Knicks, Mavericks, Cleveland Cavaliers, the Magic, and the Boston Celtics; a WNBA head coach with the New York Liberty and Washington Mystics; plus traveling all over the world as an international coach.

Richie has done it all, and he has a hilarious story for every step of his incredible journey. I don't think you'll find another guy with a résumé like Richie's—coaching junior high, high school, college, NBA, WNBA, and internationally. It's amazing, really, what he has done! And I am convinced that if Richie had better personnel at some of his NBA head-coaching stops, he would have been a super, super success on an all-time basis. But you gotta have the players. When Richie did, like when he coached the Dallas Mavericks and Orlando Magic, he won games as well as anyone and took those teams to the NBA play-offs. If he would have had some great players on a consistent basis, like some of those other guys had, there is no doubt in my mind Richie would have really been a big-time success. That's not to take away from those guys who won big, because it still takes a special quality to get people to play, to buy in and set their egos aside. Richie could do that as well as anybody. The way he can communicate with players is magical.

That doesn't happen by accident. It happens when you have a passion for players and for the game. It happens when you eat, drink, sleep, and breathe basketball. When you're a basketball junkie. When you're a lifer. That's my friend Richie Adubato.

Havin' a Ball

The Jersey Guys

We had no idea the cops were called, responding to our noisy argument that spilled onto a dark street in the middle of the night. We were young guys, macho with our opinions and mafioso in our brotherly bond. We came to call ourselves the Jersey Guys. That was a long time ago, back in the early 1960s. All these years later, we still call ourselves the Jersey Guys.

Our argument began inside a diner, growing heated as the night grew darker. We were high school basketball coaches and buddies, passionate about the game, living in the moment; and at that moment our rising voices were debating the best way to defend the pick and roll. Our props were salt and pepper shakers, representing the opposing teams, with sugar packets serving as the basket.

"You gotta go under!" one of us argued.

"Over!" someone countered.

"No, no, no. Body and under!" came another opinion.

"Trap!" yelled another. "The best way to defend the pick and roll is to trap!"

Soon, with the diner closing, we were outside in the street, grabbing metal garbage cans and dragging them across the pavement, crashing them into each other as we argued, simulating the best way to defend the pick and roll. Lights flickered on, but we didn't notice. We were too busy using our clanging props to punctuate our points.

"Coach?!"

We collectively turned and that's when we saw the flashlights. Someone had called the cops and now the cops were calling us by who we were—coaches. Not hoodlums. High school coaches. When they recognized us, and we them, and they figured out what we were doing, we all laughed and it snapped us back into reality. Some of those cops had even been coached by us. Realizing the ruckus we were causing, we called it a night. But we didn't call it a career; careers that none of us could have expected.

Within the next decade or so all of us became NBA head coaches. My best buddy, Dick Vitale, was in the street that night, his hairline only beginning to retreat. Dickie V would go on to coach the Detroit Pistons before becoming an icon as a college basketball analyst. The other guys were Hubie Brown, Mike Fratello, and I—the three of us each eventually coaching three different NBA teams, helping and hiring each other along the way. There were other fraternity members of the Jersey Guys—Al LoBalbo, Rollie Massimino, Brendan Suhr, Lou Campanelli, and Brian Hill; all of them are great coaches and even greater guys. That night in the street, though, we were still small time with big-time aspirations, and we would always say that when one of us made it we'd bring the others along.

But there was a time early in my coaching career when I didn't think I'd ever advance beyond being a high school junior varsity coach. I lived for sports and grew up playing whatever was in season. I became a good enough multi-sport athlete at New Jersey's Clifford Scott High School in East Orange, New Jersey, to earn a scholarship at nearby William Paterson University—then called Paterson State—where today I'm enshrined in the university's hall of fame for both basketball and baseball.

I got a tryout with the Philadelphia Phillies baseball team after I graduated, but nothing came of it. So I started my coaching career in the city of Paterson, during what was a racially tense time. In 1964 Paterson made national news for its race riots that lasted four furious days in August. I was in the thick of it. Not the race riots. But I knew those streets well. I was right there, deep in the inner city, teaching at a middle school by day and at night coaching jv basketball at Stevens Academy, a prep school in nearby Hoboken, which was Frank Sinatra's hometown. That first coaching job earned me $150—total. I often moonlighted as a bartender, not just to help make ends meet, but also because I enjoyed it. What happened in Paterson in 1964 wasn't a shock to me. There were always riots and skirmishes going on. The tension in those days was palpable.

After coaching two years at Stevens Academy I was coaching jv basketball at St. Joseph's in West New York, which— don't let the name fool you—was in New Jersey. One of the toughest places to play at was Union City, a real rough area known for its Cuban gangs. It wasn't unusual to need a police escort to get in and out. One night, after a win at Union City, I stopped at a bar. After I left and was stopped at a red light, a car pulled alongside of me. There were four guys inside, and I could tell they were Cuban. They kept motioning me to roll down my window, so I did. That's when a guy jumped from the backseat and punched me smack in the jaw. Almost as quickly as it happened, he was back in the car and they were speeding away, laughing.

So I did what any self-respecting Jersey guy would do. I chased them. When I saw they were going up Route 3, toward the Meadowlands, the route I had to take home anyway, I figured I'd stay in pursuit. Eventually, they pulled into a parking lot and got out, doors open, waiting for me. What the hell, I thought, and I went right after them. I had a big DeSoto with fins like a Cadillac, only bigger, and built like a tank. Guys started scrambling for safety, leaving their car doors open as they did. I accelerated, knocking the back and front doors right off the hinges from the driver's side of their car. When I turned around to take care of the other side, I noticed a couple of guys had guns aimed at me. That's all I needed to see and I floored it out of there, my tires screeching as I heard loud *pop, pop, pop* sounds.

The next day was a Saturday, and that night I was bartending. When some of my buddies came in they said, "Hey Richie, what happened? You've got bullet holes in your car."

That was Jersey, the Jersey I grew up in during the '50s and '60s.

I'd like to say that was the only time I was shot at, but it wasn't. My junior year at Paterson State, our baseball team made it to the NAIA College World Series at Sul Ross State University in Alpine, Texas. We lost our first game to Southern University, an all-black school from Baton Rouge, Louisiana. There was a kid on the team with ungodly speed. The first time he was up he dribbled a ball in front of home plate. Our catcher, Bill Fleming, had a canon for an arm. He scooped the ball and fired it on a line to the first baseman, who happened to be me. But the kid from Southern University beat the throw by several steps.

I went to the mound and told our pitcher we had to hold this guy close to first. So he threw over three times, keeping him honest. When he finally threw home, the kid took off. Again, Fleming threw a rocket, on a line all the way to second base, and I swear the kid was already dusting himself off from sliding by the time the ball got there.

In the dugout afterward, Fleming told me, "I threw a perfect throw to second and he beat it by five feet. I can't throw it any better than that. If he gets on first again and steals, I'm throwing to third."

We didn't have to worry. That same kid came up in the eighth inning and hit a home run to beat us 3–2.

Years later, when I was the Dallas Mavericks' head coach, I was on the Beau Bock sports radio talk show in Atlanta and I got to personally meet that player, who was also a guest on the show that day. By now he was known as Hall of Famer Lou

Brock. I told Lou about that game and how he'd beaten us with a homer in the eighth.

"It was the seventh," he said.

"You sure?"

Lou Brock just smiled. Athletes know. And we knew, all those years earlier as competing athletes, that we were watching greatness in its infancy.

We also knew during that NAIA World Series that we were experiencing our first real taste of racism. We heard it from the stands when we played Southern University and the n-word was flying around. Then we saw it in the next game, when we were playing Arkansas State, trying to prevent ourselves from getting eliminated. Inside their dugout was a Confederate flag and they were riding us mercilessly, this team of kids from New Jersey, calling us Yankee this and Yankee that, with some expletives slipped in. Finally, I'd had enough. Their dugout was behind first base, where I was playing.

"Hey, I don't know if you're aware of it," I said, turning toward them, "but the Civil War ended about one hundred years ago, and we beat the shit out of you guys."

Well, that did it. Now they were foaming at the mouth with their expletives. I ignored them, tossing groundballs to our infielders as our pitcher warmed up. One ball came in low from our third baseman, and I pretended that it got underneath my glove. It skipped into their dugout, scattering some of the guys. They weren't sure if it was intentional or not so they just screamed louder at me. The next throw came from our shortstop, on a line, straight for me. I let it go past my glove right into the dugout. That's when all hell broke loose. It was a brawl, a melee that even had some of the Southern University kids jumping in from the stands to help us. It took officials about twenty minutes to restore order, and when they did I saw that one of our guys had snapped in two the stick that had held their Confederate flag.

We lost that game, 8–7, eliminating us from the tournament.

5

That night, still ticked off, we went to a town bar. Sure enough, we ran into some loudmouth, redneck cowboys.

"Where you guys from with that funny accent?" one of them asked.

"New Jersey."

"New Jersey?" another redneck replied. "Shoot, we can fit New Jersey into our panhandle."

Fleming pointed at one of the guy's shoes.

"You like those boots, don't you?" he asked. "Back in Jersey we sell those things at Thom McAn for about two bucks."

Well, one word led to another, and soon we were in an all-out fight again. There were ten of us and only five of them, so we pretty much pummeled the hell out of them. Knowing that wouldn't be the end of it, we left and went across the tracks to the Mexican side of town and found a bar there. Those guys were cool and we asked one of them about heading down to the border, into Mexico. We'd heard about the whorehouses there, and the night was still young. Five guys went back to our dorm, and five of us paid one of the Mexican guys to drive us in this big Oldsmobile to the border, along a dirt road through the desert, about forty-five minutes away, and told him to wait for us after we got there.

It was about midnight and nobody on the American side was guarding the border going into Mexico. There was a short bridge going over the Rio Grande, with a five-foot barricade in the middle. We hopped it, made it to the other side, and eventually made it into the small town where the whorehouse was.

We were told it was two dollars for a regular room with a girl and three dollars for a nicer room. I chose the three-dollar room and followed her inside. She took off her clothes and went to one side of the room and knelt before a statue of the Virgin Mary, crossing herself and praying. Then she went to the other side of the room, and that's when I saw a crib. She reached in, adjusted a few things, and gently rocked it a few times. As a guy who had grown up in Catholic schools and Catholic church, that's all I needed to see. I laid the three bucks on the bed and left, hoping I had averted what I was sure would be a one-way ticket to hell.

Later, when my buddies met me outside, we headed back to the border. Not surprisingly, it wasn't so easy to get back to the United States side. They had what were called wetback patrols, and they meant business. In this case, business was the barrel of a handgun a patrol guy was holding that I swear was a foot long. It looked like something out of the Civil War.

Fleming was a tough guy. He grew up above a bar his dad owned, and he would slide down on one of those fire station poles to get from the second floor to the first.

"Bill," I told him. "I'm going to walk up to this guy and offer him money. But when I do I'm going to drop it. When he reaches down to pick it up, punch him."

It worked perfectly. When he reached down, Bill punched him, another guy kicked him, and a third guy kicked his gun about ten feet away. We sprinted for the bridge, clamored over the barricade, and ran for our lives—literally. I don't know if he was shooting at us, or to scare us, but he fired off several shots—it was the first time I heard that *pop, pop, pop* sound. I don't think I've ever run so fast, my heart about to pound out of my chest.

By the time we stopped running, we were engulfed in the blackness of night. We couldn't see our hands in front of our faces, but we could hear, and what we heard was the constant slithering and rattling of snakes. It was terrifying. We decided to walk side by side, holding hands, marching through the Texas plains. I decided I'd be the guy in the middle of us five, figuring that if someone got bit it'd be one of the guys on the end.

I don't know how many miles we trudged through that Texas plain, but we finally saw some lights and came upon a small town with a little motel. We went inside, hoping to find someone who could hook us up with a ride. Nobody was at the counter. Fleming pointed to some car keys hanging on the wall. "There's a pickup truck outside, and I bet those are the keys," he said. "I'm gonna go check." Sure enough, the keys fit and we all climbed into the pickup and took off toward Alpine, where we were supposed to be staying in our dorm rooms. When we got there, we parked the car in the middle of the town square and put a sign on it:

SORRY. KEYS ARE ON THE ROOF.

I got back to my dorm room just in time to shower and get ready for our 7 a.m. team flight back to Jersey. Little did I know that one day I'd not only become an NBA head coach in the state of Texas, but I'd also marry my second wife there, Carol, who I'm happy to say is still my wife to this day.

But thoughts of coaching in the NBA were light years away from where I was from 1960–65, when I was mired in the coaching purgatory known as junior varsity basketball. Most all my buddies, the Jersey Guys fraternity, had progressed ahead of me. Dick Vitale was the head coach at East Rutherford High, Rollie Massimino the head coach at Hillside High, and Hubie Brown the head coach at Fair Lawn High. Meanwhile, I waited and waited and waited . . .

Finally, I had the opportunity I longed for. I was coaching at Our Lady of the Valley, a parochial school in Orange, and we had just won the Essex County JV tournament, and my record in three years was 28-3. The head-coaching job was open, and our athletic director, Vinnie Carlesimo, the uncle of future college and NBA coach P. J. Carlesimo, wanted me.

"You're a terrific coach," Vinnie told me. "I'm hiring you."

I could feel my chest swelling.

"Vinnie, thanks so much," I said, shaking his hand. "I really appreciate it."

Then came the *but.*

"But," he said, "you'll have to talk to Monsignor Feeley. He'll have the final word."

Monsignor Feeley had quite a reputation. He had a passion for basketball and for winning. If you didn't win, you were gone. Once, when I was a high school player, we were in Our Lady's gym one night for a game when Monsignor Feeley introduced his head coach, Joe Olivola, to a guy named Bill Murphy, who later became a friend of mine. Olivola was an excellent coach, but unfortunately, he had just lost four of five games.

"I want you to meet the new coach," Monsignor Feeley told Olivola. "That's all. Sorry, we're firing you."

It was fifteen minutes before the game.

On the plus side of Monsignor Feeley's passion for basketball was that although Our Lady of the Valley was a small Catholic school, it had an air-conditioned gym with the capacity to hold about two thousand raucous fans.

Boy, did I want that job.

When Monsignor Feeley and I sat down to talk, I was nervous. "Coach," he began, "Vinnie's recommended you for the job. I was at the game when you guys beat Southside in Newark to win the Essex County Tournament. That was some game, an incredible win. I think we have the right guy. But first, let me ask you a couple of things."

I nodded.

"We know you played baseball in college and you went to the College World Series and you were an all-state player in high school. Well, we need a baseball coach, so would you have any problems coaching the basketball team *and* the baseball team?"

I wanted the job.

"Monsignor, no problem. I'll coach baseball. I love baseball. No problem at all."

"Okay, great," he replied. "Now let me ask you. We need a cross-country coach in the fall. Do you think you can handle that?"

I wanted the job.

"Monsignor, I ran track, but I ran low hurdles. I wasn't really associated with long-distance running. But I'll handle it."

"Wonderful," he said. "So you'll coach basketball, you'll coach baseball, and you'll coach cross country?"

"Yes."

He wasn't finished.

"You can use the gym, the brand-new gym, any time you want except Wednesday nights. Wednesday night is Bingo Night.

We make enough money off bingo to support the whole school. So on Wednesday nights you cannot practice from 7 to 10. Any other time you can use the gym."

"Fine," I said. "No problem."

"By the way," he asked, "can you say B-2 and G-4?"

Okay. I got the idea.

"We may ask you to call out the bingo numbers," the monsignor continued, "because you'll be our coach and people will like to see you up there. Do you think you can do that?"

I wanted the job.

"Whatever you want me to do, Monsignor. I can do bingo."

"Good, good," he said. "Well look, on Sunday when you come to Mass can you come to the eight o'clock Mass so you can help us with the collection?"

I nodded, knowing that all I'd need to do was walk up and down the aisles with what was then a basket at the end of a long handle. But Monsignor Feeley had special instructions.

"Before I give you the basket and you go to collect and come back, before I do that, I'm going to give you a live fly and I'm going to put it in your hand and I'm going to close your fist," he said. "When you come back with the basket and the money I'm going to open your fist and that fly better be alive."

I chuckled at the joke.

"Look," I said, "if I gotta collect on Sundays, I'll be there. No problem."

"Good," he said. "You're hired. For all that we'll pay you $500."

That was 1965, and I stayed at Our Lady of the Valley until 1969, and those were good years. I married my first wife, Trish, which led to the birth of my two children with her—Beth and Scott.

I still had bigger aspirations, however. Coaching in college was my ultimate goal. But, once again, I was lagging behind the other Jersey Guys. Not for long, though. Or so I hoped.

2

Back in College

I won a lot at the high school level, and because of that I was getting noticed. In 1969, after compiling a 76-14 record at Our Lady of the Valley, I knew I was on my way when Upsala College in East Orange, a Division III school, hired me to coach its freshman team. I immediately had a lot of success on the court with Upsala, going 42-8, but not a lot of success at home. My marriage to Trish fell apart not too many years after we married, and soon we were separated.

Part of my coaching achievements was occasionally beating a Division I school, which for a Division III team was a big deal. It opens eyes. A pair of those eyes it opened, especially because we had beaten his school, was Fordham athletic director Pete Carlesimo, who was Vinnie's brother and P.J.'s father. Pete had been aware of me for years, and he would tell me I was going to be his coach one day.

That day finally came in 1971 when his coach, Digger Phelps, took the prestigious head-coaching job at Notre Dame. I went to Fordham and interviewed with the athletic department committee, and I could tell it went well. When I got to Pete's office he was exuberant. "You're my new coach!" he said. The *New York Daily* even reported it and everything seemed set . . . until, once again, the school's monsignor entered the picture. This time I didn't even have a chance to talk to him. He nixed the hiring.

"This is a Catholic university," he said. "And as a Catholic university we can't hire a basketball coach who is separated from his wife."

It crushed me. But it also made me more determined. So I stayed at Upsala, working my tail off to get someone else to notice me. Actually, I was working my tail off at four jobs. I'd teach in Paterson's inner-city schools by day, coach freshman basketball at Upsala after school, referee Catholic Youth University league games on Sundays, and bartend on the weekends. I soon learned that bartending had extra perks beyond the tips. I would coach Upsala's freshman team from 4 p.m. to 6 p.m., and then on Friday nights, I would make sure I was bartending at Tierney's Tavern, an Irish bar in Montclair, because by 9:30 p.m. the high school games were over and the coaches would come in to throw back a few drinks and wind down. It wasn't what people would call a sports bar nowadays, but we had a couple of TVs and it was the place to go. It was also near some of the wealthier sections of Jersey, so we would get a good clientele. Yogi Berra and his wife, Carmen, were regulars, usually coming in for our cheeseburgers and fries. Phil Rizzuto stopped by a few times. Since I was a New York Yankees fan, I loved that. But it was the high school coaches, and even some of the referees, that I was most interested in. They would come in and talk about the games, and I would listen, often picking their brains. I'd ask them how so-and-so had played, were his grades getting up, and what did they think my chances were of getting him to Upsala to play for my freshman team?

After midnight I was able to give a lot of those coaches free drinks, and, especially given what high school coaches made, they were real happy about that. The stories and laughter really flowed, and everybody had a great time. By the end of the night those coaches were telling me: "Richie, I'm sending my guy to you. I like the way you handle people. I think my guy will be happy at your place, playing for you." As they heard themselves talk, they'd nod and add, "Yeah, I'm sending you my guy." Right about then, I'd smile and slide another drink in front of them. Needless to say, the more drinks I gave them, the better recruiter I was.

Thursday nights at Tierney's were a different story—a different crowd. On Thursday nights we'd get the blue-collar guys coming in after work. We'd also have the long-haired college guys coming in from Montclair State. I would refer to one group as the pickup truck guys and the other as the ponytail guys. It was oil and water.

I liked bartending, but sometimes I would be pressed into duty as a bouncer—imagine that, me with my five-foot-ten frame. But Tierney's could get rough, and some nights we needed four or five bouncers. Well, this one Thursday night was one of those nights. The pickup truck and ponytail guys were mouthing off at each other. A couple of shoves led to a couple of punches, and pretty soon it was an all-out brawl that took the police to finally get it under control. I was in the middle of it, trying to break it up. In the jumble of bodies and blows, I didn't realize it, but I was kicked in the jaw.

I had a vacation scheduled to the Caribbean island of Martinique that I went on, and the whole time my jaw was hurting. When I returned home, I went to the dentist, thinking I had an abscessed tooth. When he X-rayed my mouth, he discovered a broken jaw.

"It's lined up well, though," he said. "I think if you're careful, it should heal itself."

A week later, with the pain getting worse, I went back to him. He X-rayed again and saw that it wasn't healing, so he wired it shut. When your jaw is wired shut, you're constantly aware that you can't talk, but every once in a while you forget. One of those times was at practice, when I thought the guys weren't hustling; they were just going through the motions on a drill. The more I watched, the angrier I got.

"You guys gotta start hustling!!!" I screamed.

At that, all the wires blew out of my jaw and the guys busted out laughing. I wasn't laughing, though. It was some of the worst pain I've ever felt.

Although some of my recruiting came greased with free liquor, most of my recruiting was done the traditional way, which can still be an adventure when it comes to college basketball. I remember recruiting one kid named Dyran Thomas, who had dominated an All-Star Game that featured the best high school players from New Jersey and New York. Dyran had freakish talent, but the problem was keeping him in school. USC in Los Angeles wanted him and sent him to junior college to get eligible, but it didn't work out. Dyran spent a month or two at a couple of junior colleges, and before long he was back home in Newark. That's when I saw him playing in a game, this six-foot-six and 250-pound physical specimen, dominating the boards, blocking shots. Afterward, I approached him.

"Dyran, how you doin'?" I said. "I'm Richie Adubato, coach of Upsala College, right up the street. I know you came back home. A lot of players like to go away, but then they feel that they'd rather experience playing at home where their families and their friends can see them."

"Yeah, yeah," he mumbled, nodding. "I'm thinking about coming back and playing in this area."

"Great," I said. "We're a Division III school. We're about twenty minutes from Newark, from your house. Maybe you can take a look. I know there are gonna be a lot of schools interested. I'll give you a call and send you some information."

I knew he lived on South Tenth Street in Newark, and I knew the area because I had lived in Newark until I was ten years old. So I went to visit him. He lived on the third floor of a three-story building. I walked up the three flights, knocked at the door, and his mother answered. I stood there, peeking in, telling her who I was and why I'd come.

"Is Dyran here?" I asked.

"Yeah. He's upstairs."

I looked around, but I didn't see an "upstairs."

"Dy-ran!" she shouted, stretching the syllables as she let me follow her inside. "Dyyy-rannn! There's a basketball coach here to see you."

"I'm comin'."

It sounded like a voice descending from the heavens. I looked around and then up, and when I did I saw a rope lowering from a hole in the ceiling.

"I'm comin' right down, or do you wanna come up?"

What the heck, I thought.

"I'll come up," I said.

I climbed the rope through the ceiling and into the attic, where Dyran slept. His bedroom furniture was old car seats and a beat-up couch and a couple of ratty chairs. We talked for a while, and eventually I took him to visit the campus.

"We're gonna need to get your grades, your transcripts," I told him.

I called one junior college in California, but they said Dyran was only there a month, not long enough to generate any grades. They referred me to another junior college in California, and when I called they said he'd only attended two months, not long enough to generate any grades, either. But then I learned he had attended a prep school in North Carolina, one known for producing great players who went on to play for some major universities around the country. I called the coach, who was also the athletic director.

"I need Dyran Thomas's transcripts," I told him. "I'm trying to get him into Upsala College."

"What transcripts do you want?" he asked. "Do you want the A transcript, the B transcript, or the C transcript?"

Without bothering to ask the difference, and figuring that A was better than C, I automatically said, "I'll take the A."

"Okay," he said. "The A is three thousand dollars, the B is two thousand, and the C is one thousand."

This was revelatory to me.

"I'm gonna have to get back to you," I said.

I got a hold of a guy named Ted Sabarese, who graduated from Upsala and was our biggest donor. Anytime we needed help, we knew we could go to Ted. I told him what the deal was. He nodded.

"Tell him we'll take the B transcript, and I'll send him the two thousand dollars."

I called the athletic director back.

"Okay, we're good to go," I said. "We'll take the B transcript."

He paused for a moment and then said, "I have to tell you that since we last talked, the B transcript has gone up to three thousand dollars."

"I'll get back with you," I said.

I never did. I didn't want any part of him anymore. I decided to take Dyran for his GED, a high school equivalency exam. Being a teacher, I knew where all the locations were. Dyran took the test—and failed. Three times I took him to take the test—and three times he failed. And I even had tutors helping him. Finally, after the fourth try, we got Dyran academically eligible, and he was a great player for us. We started the season with a string of victories, beating some very good teams, even some Division I schools. We were invited to an all-Lutheran tournament in Minneapolis, which featured schools from all over the country.

"Listen, guys," I told our team, "we're a Lutheran school and all the other schools are Lutheran. We have to be careful. We can't be getting into arguments with the officials. No cursing, because people are not gonna like it. So I'm telling you again, we have to be careful."

During our first game, Dyran got a couple of quick fouls, bad calls against him, and soon enough he was in foul trouble. Early in the second half, he fouled out, and when he did he laid the basketball down in the middle of the court and sat on it, his face etched with defiance. Dyran was like a smaller Shaquille O'Neal, and he wouldn't move.

One of the refs came over. "Coach, your player will not give us the ball, and if he doesn't give us the ball soon, you're going to forfeit the game."

My assistant coach was Ron Rothstein, who later became an NBA and WNBA head coach.

"Ron," I said, "go get the ball from Dyran."

He looked at me as if I had just grown an extra head.

"Man, I'm not going out there," he said. "You recruited the guy. You go get it from him."

"You're supposed to be my assistant," I said. "You can't help me out here?"

"You know him better than me," he said. "You do it."

So I went out and told Dyran that if he didn't give the refs the ball we'd have to forfeit. "But if you don't want to, that's okay," I added. "It's a double-elimination tournament, so if we lose we're still in it."

Dyran got up, gave me the ball, and walked off the court.

We lost that game by a point but still made it to the finals, where we lost to a very good team.

As great as Dyran was, he didn't like to practice. Many times he'd just disappear into the whirlpool or somewhere else, and it was ruining the chemistry on the team. It upset a lot of his teammates. Eventually, I had to throw him off the team, which led to a couple of other guys, buddies of Dyran's, to quit.

Five years later, when I was an assistant coach with the New York Knicks in the early 1980s, we were playing the Philadelphia 76ers, and I saw Dyran in the stands. I recognized him right away. After the game, he came over and wanted to talk.

"Coach, I gotta apologize," he said. "I was a kid, and I did a lot of crazy things, as most kids do. But after I left you I signed a pro contract to play in Venezuela. I've been playing there for four years."

"That's great, Dyran," I said. "I'm so happy for you. I'm glad you got the chance to play professional basketball."

There was never a dull moment, though, coaching Division III college basketball, getting guys who had the talent, but not the academics. One of my players was a kid named Calvin Tillman, who was good enough that he almost made the Detroit Pistons, but we had a hard time keeping him eligible. Calvin was the kind of player who never ceased to surprise me with what he'd do off the court.

One time, after returning late from a game, we had to stay at the Marriott by the Newark airport. The next day, the general manager pulled me aside.

"Coach, I need to tell you that there's nothing left in room 36," he said. "There are no pillowcases, no lamps, no throw rugs, no pictures on the wall . . ."

"Let me go check," I said.

It turned out room 36 was Calvin's room. As we boarded the team bus, I saw him carrying a bag full of stuff. I called him over.

"Calvin, what's in those bags?"

"Coach . . . coach . . . I'm havin' a party this weekend, and I don't have any furniture in my house. I'm just borrowing some of the things from the room."

"Uh, Calvin, you can't do that."

Once again, I called Ted Sabarese. He told me to tell the hotel general manager that we'd take care of it.

Calvin was one of the players I brought in under the minority program, which was an effort by Upsala to reach out and bring in kids from the inner city. Those were the kids you especially wanted to do well and make a good impression for the school. One time, there was a game that our college president came to, and he was sitting near the bench. Calvin had gotten three early fouls, so I took him out. The one thing about Calvin was that he was a great teammate, always encouraging guys from the bench. On this particular night he was exhorting the guys on the court to move their feet, except that wasn't the way he was saying it.

"Mooda feets! Mooda feets!" he kept shouting.

Oh my god, I thought. We have the college president here and he's hearing this kid shout, "Mooda feets!" I quickly called timeout and got Calvin back in the game. I figured it was better to risk him fouling out than it was for our president to hear him say, "Mooda feets!"

Another time, we were in the locker room getting ready for a big game and I looked around and didn't see Calvin. Then I heard the shower running. I peeked around the corner and there was Calvin, taking a shower *before* the game.

"Calvin, whaddaya doin' taking a shower before the game?" I asked.

"Coach, I like to take a shower before the game because it gets too crowded in here after the game."

That was Calvin, and that was the plight of a small-time Division III basketball coach.

I had a lot of success at Upsala, winning one hundred games and losing fifty-three, which was good enough for a .654 winning percentage. But there was one person who was unhappy with all the success I was having, and I was shocked to learn that it was my athletic director, a guy named Fred Wieboldt. At first I couldn't figure out why. Then it became apparent. He was the basketball coach before me, and I followed his mediocre career—and I'm being generous when I call it mediocre—with a lot of success. Because of that, he was jealous. If he had only stopped at being jealous, I would have been fine with that. But Wieboldt reported me to the NCAA with bogus and nitpicky infractions. It blindsided me. I was sitting in my little office one day toward the end of a season, and a guy named Jim Delany showed up. I'd known Jim for years, going back to when he was a star player at St. Benedict's Prep and I was coaching at Our Lady of the Valley.

"Jim, how are you?" I said when I saw him. "What are you doing here?"

"I'm with the NCAA now."

"Wow. That's terrific."

"We're here to investigate you."

"Investigate me? Come on, Jim. I've known you forever. I know your father. We both coached against each other in high school. I watched you grow up."

"I really don't want to be here. But we got a letter from your athletic director, and in that letter he said that you guys had violated some rules."

"*My* athletic director sent you a letter?"

"Yup, and we have a list of the rules you broke."

"Jim, do you realize we're Division III? We're Division III

and a terrific academic school. We're not Division I. We're not playing for national championships. We're not on TV. I would think there's a lot of work you guys have to do in that Division I area. Not naming names here, but I happen to know a lot about the recruiting world and what goes on."

"Yeah, I'm sorry, Richie. I really am sorry, but this is what it's all about."

"Okay. How about letting me know what the violations are?"

Delaney honed in on my man Ted Sabarese, whose company, Ultimate Computer Corp., had made him a multimillionaire many times over. Sabarese helped us in a lot of ways, mostly little things here and there. Sometimes he'd get us a private bus so we could set our own times for departures and returns. What Delaney wanted to know about was the jobs Sabarese was providing for some of my players on Saturday mornings.

"We've contacted the Upsala president," he continued, "and we're going to sit down with him and some faculty members and the athletic director, and we're going to call you in and we're going to try to get to the bottom of this."

He gave me a list of things they were investigating. That was upsetting enough. But what really upset me was that my own athletic director had set this up.

When I looked into the charges, I could see they weren't valid. One charge was that Sabarese was paying our players too much money for the work they were doing. But we were able to prove that their hourly wage was exactly what the average employee would earn. The second charge was that we did not eat at the school cafeteria, but rather at an off-campus restaurant. NCAA rules stated that if you ate off campus you couldn't pay more than what you would pay on campus. The restaurant was owned by a buddy of mine, and what we paid to eat there was *less* than what we would have had to pay in the school cafeteria. The third charge was that my players were taking summer classes at Essex Community College in order to stay eligible, and there was some suspicion that some funny business was going on. But when they checked the transcripts, everything was on the up and up.

Before we all met with the NCAA, I was sitting in a room with Wieboldt, and he turned to me and said, "You know, you really shouldn't have any hard feelings here, because I'm just doing my job."

"No hard feelings," I said. "You're doing your job. You gotta do what you gotta do. You think you're doing right doing this. That's fine. That's why we're clearing the air and having this meeting."

When we finally all sat down, we were able to prove that all the charges were invalid, so they were dismissed. During that meeting, however, I had the pleasure of mentioning that if the athletic director felt that eating at a restaurant off campus was so wrong, why did he often eat with us there? It really made him look bad, and also revealed his motives.

When the meeting was over, Sabarese asked me what I thought about what had happened.

"I'm not too happy with what Fred did," I told him. "I really think he should lose his athletic directorship. Maybe he should become head of intramurals." I mentioned intramurals because they started at 5 p.m. and went to 8 p.m., a miserable assignment usually reserved for someone just starting out. I knew Sabarese, who was probably the biggest donor the school had, could make it happen. But would he?

Sure enough, not too long after that, Wieboldt, who was not only the athletic director but had the cushy job of golf coach, was relieved of those duties and reassigned as the head of intramurals.

One night not too long after that, I was walking by the gym; it was a sweltering evening, at least ninety degrees. I saw Fred, supervising the intramurals, beads of sweat on his face. I looked at him and he looked at me.

"Hey, Fred," I said, "no hard feelings."

It was a small-time thing for Fred to do to me. And I was tired of the small time. I was ready for bigger and better things.

3

Closing in on the Big Time

It seemed as if I was living two lives, with one foot in the public school system and the other foot in the burgeoning world of basketball. By day I was teaching at tough middle schools in Paterson, New Jersey. I spent eighteen years doing that, from 1960–78. It never seemed to get easier, although I loved working with kids, especially the black kids from the inner city. For whatever reason, I could relate to them—probably because I wanted to. I came to understand and appreciate the culture of black America—their family structure, what's important to them, the problems they deal with—and I enjoyed it very much.

But it wasn't easy.

It helped that I was young and still an athlete, still actively involved. I even played in a semi-pro basketball league in Paterson. I could beat most every kid one-on-one in the school gym, and they respected that.

The toughest school I taught at was School No. 4 on River Street in Paterson. The first day I was there, there were at least four fistfights. A couple of other faculty guys, who were also former basketball and football players, and I were always in the middle of them, breaking them up. Those kids saw from day one that we were as tough as they were, that we meant business, and most importantly, that we stuck together. That latter point was critical to keeping things under control. Even still, when you're in that classroom alone, you'd better know what you're doing. Those kids were always testing your limits. And like anyone, I had mine.

One day, one of the female students told me something that made me feel good. It also made me laugh. "You have a very good reputation as a teacher," she said. "Very easygoing. But we all know that if your face turns red, you better get under the desk."

Eventually, I was transferred to School No. 28, also in Paterson, and just as rough. My last year there, they placed four problem kids into my eighth-grade class, likely because they believed I could handle them. These four kids—three of them black and one Latino—had mugged a homeless guy the previous summer. When they discovered he had no money, they poured gasoline on him and set him on fire. Because they were fifteen, they weren't prosecuted. Instead, they gave them to me. I saw right away that in the mornings they were confronting other kids as they came into school, shaking them down for money. I put a stop to that. I also put them in the front row of my class, so I could keep an eye on them.

That was my day job, my life in inner-city public schools. And then there was my other life, the one that involved a bouncing ball. I wasn't just coaching the team at Upsala College, I was working summer camps, hobnobbing with some great talent.

The main camp I worked was the one that Howard Garfinkel and Will Klein started in 1966 called the Five-Star Basketball Camp. We just called it Five-Star, and it was a summertime mecca for great coaches and great players, and it became legendary. Through the years, the list of players who came through Five-Star reads like a who's-who list of basketball greats— guys like Michael Jordan, Isiah Thomas, Moses Malone, Alonzo Mourning, Patrick Ewing, LeBron James, Kevin Durant, Stephen Curry, Carmelo Anthony, Chris Paul, and Tim Duncan, among others. And through the years, among the coaches who coached and lectured, there were legends like John Calipari, Chuck Daly, Rick Pitino, Dean Smith, Jim Boeheim, Jim Calhoun, Lute Olson, Jack Ramsay, Al McGuire, Denny Crum, Mike Krzyzewski, and Roy Williams, just to name a few. Five-Star is where I first met this young, intense, vulgar, black-haired basketball coach known as Bobby Knight.

This was the late sixties, and Knight was a young guy coaching Army at West Point, where one of his young players was a kid named Mike Krzyzewski. Garf, as we all called Garfinkel, introduced Knight one day and said he was going to instruct the camp on a drill.

With that look that could burn a hole through a cinder block, Knight addressed the campers, barking at them, "The first thing I wanna do is find out how many of you are tough enough to play the defense we play at West Point. So when I blow the whistle I want everybody in the center jump circle." I looked and there must have been 150 guys. The whistle blew and they all ran for the circle, all of them trying to prove how tough they were—and there were some tough guys in the group. They were climbing on each other, pushing, shoving, elbowing. I looked at Garf, and he looked apoplectic.

Suddenly Knight blew the whistle again and ordered the campers back to the sideline. "Okay," Knight growled, "we're going to work on the defensive stance." He was going through various techniques and footwork and then, in typical Knight fashion, he broke it down in a way I've never forgotten—and I expect neither did the campers: "You've gotta pretend you're in the woods," he said. "You're in the woods and you've gotta take a shit. There's no outhouse, so you gotta do it in the woods. You've gotta make sure you're down enough in your stance so that when you take your shit you don't get anything on your feet or ankles."

That was Bobby Knight.

Five-Star Camp was the place to be. Young coaches, veteran coaches, rising talent, NBA players . . . they all came to Five-Star. One of the most amazing guys I ever saw there was Calvin Murphy, who went on to have a Hall of Fame career in the NBA. I remember once he got a standing ovation from about

250 campers after one of his lectures—except it wasn't what I would call a pure lecture. Calvin put on a show. At only five feet nine, Calvin could still jump out of the gym. And shoot out the lights. And run. And dribble. Goodness, could that man dribble a basketball. He would talk for a little bit and then, while dribbling two basketballs, he'd ask for the fastest guys in camp. We had some lightning-quick guys. Calvin, while dribbling two basketballs, would chase them around the court. Once he touched a kid they were out. There were three guys, and he got the first two and then went after the third. Dribbling the two balls, he backed the camper into a corner and then, in one fluid motion, he slid and, while still dribbling, touched the kid on the foot and said, "You're out."

Another drill he would do was stand at the free-throw line and announce to all these great players at camp that he was going to throw the ball against the backboard, catch it on the rebound, and dribble the full length of the court and dunk it.

"How many dribbles do you think it will take me?" he would ask.

The campers, most all of them athletic and well over six feet, would look at this five-foot-nine guy and shout:

"Eight!"

"Seven!"

Maybe one wise guy would shout, "Six!"

Calvin would then throw the ball off the backboard and catch it in the air right around the top of the key, but because of his hang time, he'd land somewhere between the top of the key and half court. It would then take him only *four* dribbles before he would launch himself from just inside the foul line to thunder home a dunk. The place would erupt. Guys would be jumping up and down, shouting and applauding. That was Calvin. He had a whole bagful of tricks that wowed the camp, and year after year he was always a favorite.

One year at camp, though, Garf came to me at eight in the morning and said, "Calvin is not making it."

"Wow," I said. "Who you gonna get to take his place?"

Garf thought for a moment. Calvin was always the main lecturer, so replacing him was no small task. "Well, Dean Smith is here," he said. "Digger Phelps is here. There are a number of big program coaches here. I'll see if one of them could do the lecture."

"Good idea," I said.

Two hours later, Garf came back to me. "Richie, nobody wants to do this. None of them want to take Calvin's place."

"I can understand that," I said.

"How about you doing the lecture?" he said.

"Replace Calvin!" I practically shouted, shaking my head. "I've seen what he can do. There's no way I'm gonna go out there and make a fool of myself by trying to take his place. No way, Garf. I can't do that."

"Okay, okay," he said. "Let me try a few more coaches."

An hour later, Garf came back to me. "Richie, I'm begging you. I'm begging you. You gotta do the lecture for Calvin."

I didn't know what to say. I went back to my cabin and sat there thinking. As I was telling myself that I couldn't do it, a light bulb went off. I was a small-college coach who, up until then, kind of blended in the background. This was my opportunity to showcase myself in front of a bunch of major college coaches. I jotted down a couple of things I'd been doing throughout the week at my camp station, stuff that I knew went over well with the campers.

Still, I don't think I've ever been more nervous. There were about 250 players sitting around the court, with all eyes on me. Off to the side were my fellow coaches, and I could feel their examining eyes. Somehow, someway, I not only made it through my lecture, I got a standing ovation. As I did, I thought: This is great exposure.

My best exposure, though, was with my fellow Jersey Guys— buddies like Dick Vitale, Hubie Brown, and Rollie Massimino. We all had our own camps during those years. Vitale's camp was the same week as mine, and one day I needed a speaker, so I called him.

"Dick, my guest speaker bailed on me. You have one for me today."

"Yeah, but if you're gonna use my speaker, we gotta split the cost."

"Sure," I agreed.

I was ecstatic when I learned that Dick was sending over Bob Love, one of the NBA's great players for the Chicago Bulls. I eagerly shook Bob's hand when he arrived and told him I would introduce him and that he'd be on for about an hour. "Do some shooting drills since you're such a great shooter, and then explain how you were able to come out of rural Louisiana and a small college all the way to becoming an NBA star."

He nodded.,

A little while later, with all the campers gathered around, I gave Bob a great introduction. He stepped forward, and out from his mouth came, "Uh . . . uh . . . g-g-good . . . to-to . . . be-be-be . . . h-h-here."

I was mortified. I had no idea that Bob Love had such a speech impediment, such a bad stuttering problem. My guest speaker couldn't even speak.

I immediately jumped up and pulled my three best shooters at the camp onto the court. I had them scrimmage against Bob, and of course he beat all three. I had him look at and evaluate the types of drills we were running to see if he approved, and of course he did, adding a few little tidbits here and there; things he could demonstrate without doing a lot of talking. At the end I thanked him for coming.

Then I called Vitale.

"What are you doing?" I demanded. "I asked you to send me a guest speaker, and you send me someone who can't speak, and you don't even warn me!"

Vitale just laughed. That was Dickie V.

As for Bob Love, after a stellar eleven-year NBA career that saw him become a three-time All-Star, his stuttering became so bad he couldn't find work. At one point he was practically destitute, bussing tables and washing dishes at a Nordstrom department store restaurant in Seattle for $4.45 an hour. When none other than John Nordstrom, grandson of the store's founder, recognized what was going on, he paid for Love to take speech therapy classes. He moved up in the company, eventually becoming its corporate spokesman. In 1991 the Bulls hired him as their director of community affairs. Today, the guy who couldn't speak at my camp is a motivational speaker.

Meanwhile, my friendship with Dick Vitale, which would become a lifelong friendship, was growing stronger. When he got the head-coaching job at the University of Detroit, he asked me to come and be his assistant. I went to check it out. I don't know what it was about my career up until that point, but all my opportunities seemed to come in rough inner-city areas, and the University of Detroit was no different. This university was in downtown Detroit—a particularly bad area in a city that didn't have too many safe places to begin with.

Before practice, a couple of guys walked right in off the street and into the gym. These were scary looking guys who looked like they might be carrying a concealed weapon. There was something menacing about them. Without saying a word, they went straight for the carts with all the basketballs and wheeled them right out of the gym. Nobody said a word.

Finally, I spoke.

"Dick, obviously I appreciate the offer. But I'm gonna have a great team this upcoming season at Upsala, and I'll do everything I can to help you get some players, but I think I'm gonna stay back home."

Vitale understood. And then he went to work, completely transforming the program into a winner. In four years he took a nondescript university and went 78-30, including a twenty-one-game winning streak in 1977, when he had the team ranked in the top ten. It was exciting times for Dick—so exciting that one time he called and woke me at four in the morning to tell me how he'd just beaten Marquette University and the legendary coach Al McGuire. Dick was talking so fast he was tripping over his words, and all I wanted to do was go back to sleep.

Dickie V became an icon in Detroit. And then he became the head coach of the NBA's Detroit Pistons. That's when he asked me again to come to Detroit and help him coach. This time I couldn't turn him, or the big time, down.

4

Motormouth City

They say the postman always rings twice. Well, so does Dick Vitale. And I'm glad he did. After turning down his offer of assistant coach at the University of Detroit, Vitale called me again in 1978, and again he tried to woo me to Detroit, only this time there was a twist.

"They're going to name me head coach of the Detroit Pistons," he told me over the phone. "Come be one of my assistants."

I couldn't answer *yes* fast enough. I'd been waiting to get to the big time, but this was bigger than anything I could've ever dreamed. The NBA. I'd been in the game for eighteen years, coaching junior high school kids, high school kids, college kids, never thinking there was another rung on the ladder. And now the NBA was opening its door for me. It was a Jersey Guys offer I couldn't refuse, and I couldn't get to Detroit fast enough.

My first day at the Pistons' facility, Vitale was showing me around, and we walked into the trainer's room. Sitting in the whirlpool was the six-foot-eleven frame of Bob Lanier, one of the league's great centers who was in the prime of his Hall of Fame career.

"Bob," Vitale said, "I'd like you to meet our new assistant coach, Richie Adubato."

Lanier didn't move. He just glanced at me sideways.

"Great," he said, "another white guy who's going to tell us how to play basketball."

"That's it, I quit," I said, playfully overdramatizing my voice. "I'm going back to New Jersey, where I get respect."

It got a laugh from Lanier, and we became fast friends, occasionally going out together. He'd take me to the downtown restaurants and bars, where most of the time I was the only white guy. But because I was with Bob, there was never a problem. They loved Bob, and I was Bob's friend. All he had to say was, "That's my man. Make sure you treat him with respect." And that was it. I was gold after that. Lanier also had a dry sense of humor. One time, we were at a basketball banquet in Canada. Beforehand we were having dinner, when Lanier looked at me and deadpanned, "I'm gonna go to the men's room, but there are some short guys outside and I'm worried about them."

I played along.

"Bob, you're six feet eleven, 250 pounds," I said. "What are you worried about?"

"A lot of people are looking for notoriety. And they're looking at me funny. They might come at me with that karate stuff. One of them might get lucky and it could be a feather in their cap."

"One thing is for sure," I said. "I have your knees covered. Because keeping those knees safe means Dick and I have a chance to win. So you can count on one thing—I'll be in front of you protecting those knees."

He laughed. We had a good relationship that way. I didn't mind being his straight man.

In spite of having a great player like Lanier, we were a bad team. First-time coaches in the NBA don't normally get plum jobs. There was a reason why they hired Vitale out of the University of Detroit, and it was because the Pistons finished their 1977–78 season with a 38-44 record, which got two coaches fired—Herb Brown during the season and interim coach Bob Kauffman after the season. Because of his success with the University of Detroit, Vitale was viewed as a savior, and he worked the goodwill the fans were buying into. Before the season, he and I traveled all over Michigan, speaking to fans wherever we could. Vitale even came up with a bumper sticker that he'd hand out to people. It said: Re-VITALE-ize the Pistons. But Dick didn't stop there. There were times we would pull up in front of Tigers Stadium before an MLB game and Vitale would throw Pistons basketballs to people and then run around handing out those bumper stickers. Nobody worked harder at promoting Pistons basketball than Dickie V did.

I joke that in the small print of the contract I signed, it said that I had to chauffer Vitale around. Not that I minded. In fact, if you ever sat in the passenger's seat when Dick was driving, you would want to be his chauffeur, too. But what Vitale lacked behind the wheel, he more than made up for as a coach. A lot of people today don't realize just how good a basketball coach Dick Vitale was.

Vitale poured everything he had into that team. He tried to fire them up like they were a group of college players, but that didn't really work. The first team meeting we had, Vitale was working the locker room, pacing around and telling the guys, "We're gonna change the culture here and we're gonna do it with hard work and dedication and a lot of desire!" The more he talked, the more worked up he got. Trying to punctuate a point, he kicked a box of basketballs. Then, figuring he'd make a grand exit, Dick hit the door out of the locker room as if he were going to bust through it. Problem was, it was chained from the outside. The door gave a few inches before bouncing Dick back across the locker room, staggering him. Ron Rothstein, who was one of our scouts and later became an NBA head coach, looked at me and I at him. Then Dick laughed, and that made everyone laugh. He was a good sport about it. Once we got outside, Dick said, "Well, I guess I showed them who the boss is going to be around here."

That was Dick. Passionate. Unfiltered. And a little crazy. The guy you see today doing ESPN broadcasts of college basketball games is that same guy I've always known. It isn't an act. That's Dick Vitale. When he's enthusiastic about something, he's *enthusiastic*.

There were times when being an NBA head coach came in handy, especially when it came to meeting celebrities. While Dick and I were coaching in Detroit, Frank Sinatra came to the city for a concert. Being a couple of Jersey guys, we knew we not only had to go to the concert, but we also had to meet Sinatra. We knew that our pal UNLV head coach Jerry Tarkanian was close with Sinatra because of the Vegas connection. Back in the day, Tark used to run with Sinatra, Sammy Davis Jr., and Dean Martin and was practically a member of the Rat Pack. So we called him up. Tark called Sinatra's buddy Jilly Rizzo, and Jilly arranged for us to meet Sinatra the afternoon before that night's show.

Vitale and I had a Pistons jersey made that had Sinatra's name and the number one on the back. When we got to the hotel suite, Jilly let us in and told us, "Frank'll be right out. Tark called and said you were okay guys; that you're both Jersey guys."

When Sinatra came out to meet us, he was great. We gave him the Pistons' jersey and he seemed genuinely ecstatic. The conversation flowed, and we were thrilled to meet him. After a while, he said, "Guys, you'll have to excuse me, but I've got to get my nap in. I've left you tickets for the show. I hope you have a good time." We told him we understood, no problem, and thanked him for his time and for the tickets.

The concert that night was at a venue in Clarkston, Michigan, called the Pine Knob Music Theatre. When we showed our tickets to the usher and he took us to our seats, we saw that they were good but not great. I was okay with it, but Vitale being Vitale, he put the force of his winsome personality in motion. Once they realized who he was, and that we had been with Sinatra earlier that day, we were upgraded to some really nice seats. Needless to say, we had a great time. That's Dickie V. People just can't help being won over by his wonderfully exuberant personality.

In so many ways on the basketball court, Vitale's outsized way of doing things immediately came through that first season. It was Ball Day one night at the Silverdome in Pontiac, Michigan, and they handed out small basketballs to the fans when they entered the arena. We were winning fairly easily, and Vitale turned to me during a timeout:

"I think they need more balls," he said.

I looked at him quizzically. "Didn't they get enough?" I asked.

"No. I think they need some more."

At that, he reached under the bench and pulled out a big bag of those little basketballs. He dragged it to the front of the scorer's table, with the game going on, and proceeded to dribble them and then throw them into the stands. People went wild. I couldn't help but shake my head and laugh. We were playing the Denver Nuggets, who were coached by longtime NBA lifer Doug Moe. Finally, I ran behind Dick and tried to rein him in. That's when I saw the expression on Doug Moe's face and knew he obviously wasn't pleased. I told Dick later, "You just made your first NBA coaching enemy. You wouldn't be too happy either if you were getting beat by 25 points and the other coach was throwing basketballs into the stands right in front of your bench."

Dick tried everything that season, motivating and coaching his butt off, but when you have a bad team, and then you have injuries, you're not going to win too many ballgames, and we didn't. That first season the Pistons regressed from 38-44 the previous year to 30-52. Unfortunately, we lost Bob Lanier that season for fifty-three games due to ongoing knee injuries, and you just don't replace superstar centers like Lanier.

That off-season, I learned that our owner, Bill Davidson, was working on a trade for Bob McAdoo. I knew McAdoo was a great scorer and could score from anywhere—with the added advantage of being six feet nine. But us Jersey Guys were all indoctrinated in defense, and I knew we weren't going to get that from McAdoo. I expressed my concern to Vitale.

"He's a great scorer, we all know that," I said. "But remember, he's not gonna guard. He's not gonna play defense. He is what he is—a prolific scorer. He doesn't fit what we're trying to do here."

"I know, I know," Vitale said, "but Davidson wants him."

When the trade went down before the 1979–80 season—we essentially sent M. L. Carr and two first round draft picks to the Boston Celtics—I was in New Jersey. Vitale called me at about eleven at night. McAdoo happened to live in a very wealthy area of Bergen County.

"I want you to go up to his house," Vitale said. "I want you to go up there right now and tell him what a great team we're going to have."

"Dick, it's eleven o'clock."

"No, no, you need to go now and tell him what a great team we're going to have."

How do you say *no* to Dickie V? You can't. Before I realized it, I was driving up to this beautiful suburban area. They had gaslights, so it was dimly lit. I couldn't see much. McAdoo's house was off the road, behind gates. Just as I was trying to figure out how I was going to get past those gates, I heard the ferocious sound of barking dogs.

I jumped back in my car and drove to a phone booth.

"Dick, look, I can't go in there. There are dogs barking and—"

"You gotta go in! You gotta go in there and tell him. He'll be so happy to know that we're going to have a great team and how much we need him."

"Dick, I can't go back there tonight. Tell you what, I'll get a motel room and I'll be there at seven in the morning. I'll get there first thing and tell him how much we're going to need him."

"Okay, okay. But we need to get him to Detroit tomorrow. I've got a parade set up, and a car dealer is going to give him a big Cadillac. You've gotta get him here."

I got up at six the next morning, got dressed, and pulled up to McAdoo's house just as his wife was coming out, taking two of their kids to school. I told her who I was and why I was there.

35

"Just go right in and make yourself comfortable," she said. "When Bob gets up you can talk to him."

She went in and I gingerly followed, waiting to hear any sound of barking dogs. But I didn't. I just sat there in the living room and waited. And waited and waited and waited. About ten thirty, McAdoo came downstairs. Before he had a chance to say anything, I extended my hand, "Hi Bob, I'm Richie Adubato, Dick Vitale's assistant coach with the Detroit Pistons."

He looked at me as if I had an extra head, so I kept talking.

"You're our new acquisition and we're so excited about this team and having you on it. We're really gonna roll with you part of that front line and the guards we have and the young kids we have. It should be a terrific season now that you're with us. Why don't we go to the diner down the road and talk over breakfast."

I broke free while we were eating and called Dick.

"You need to get him out here today," he said.

"I'll see what I can do."

When I told McAdoo we wanted him to fly to Detroit that same day, he wouldn't hear it.

"Absolutely not. There's no way I can do that. I haven't even talked to my agent yet. I don't see myself getting out there for another four or five days."

I called Vitale back and he was crushed.

"I did what I could do," I told him.

We started the 1979–80 season 4-4 before heading to Milwaukee to play a very good Bucks team that featured players like Marques Johnson, Sidney Moncrief, and Junior Bridgeman. Right from the opening jump ball we were getting blown out and Vitale was calling timeouts like crazy, but nothing worked and we quickly fell behind by 20 points. Vitale was screaming at the guys, wanting to know where their heads were at. Nothing worked, and we got killed.

Heading back to the hotel, Dick was livid. We sat there in the lobby and he was ranting about how the guys "didn't play hard" and "didn't give their all" and on and on and on. Finally, at about three in the morning I said, "Dick, c'mon. Let's go to bed. The one thing you can't worry about in the NBA is one game. This one's over. We've got another game in five days. We've gotta travel. We'll be ready for the next one. Let's go."

I was up early the next morning, at about seven thirty, and when I went down to the lobby, Lanier was there, wearing a worried look. "Richie, Dick's very upset. He's in the coffee shop, really upset at the guys about how bad they played and how they disgraced the Piston uniform and how that's why we lost so many games last year."

Dick is such a competitor and so passionate, and because of that he really took losses hard. It ate at him. I knew that about my friend, so when I got to the coffee shop, I reminded him that it was okay and that we needed to move forward. "We've got another game coming up," I said. "We'll correct the mistakes we made in practice." He was okay after that. Before we boarded the bus, though, he picked up a newspaper, and there, smeared across the sports page, was the headline: "Pistons Re-VITALE-ize Bucks." That did it. Dick let the players have it again, pacing the aisle, telling the team, "You guys have no pride! Nobody here has any dedication! Nobody here knows how to win!"

We lost the next game, and the next game, and the next game after that. And then we lost Dick Vitale. After a 4-8 start in just his second season as a head coach, he was fired. I hurt so badly for him. Almost immediately afterward, he was contacted by a fledgling cable sports network called ESPN. They were enamored with Dick's outsized personality and wanted him to be a color commentator on college basketball games. Vitale didn't want to hear it.

"Absolutely no way!" he said. "I know nothing about TV. I want to get back to where I belong and where my spirit belongs."

His wife Lorraine talked him into it, though.

"Go on TV and have some fun," she told him.

So he did, and his broadcasting career began on December 5, 1979. From the get-go Dick kept insisting that this was only until he got a coaching job. All these years later he's still with ESPN, an icon on the network and in college basketball, with a contract that takes him through 2022.

As for me, when Vitale got fired I stood in the back of the news conference, wondering what my own fate would be. Afterward, I went over and talked to Lanier.

"Bob, what do you think is going to happen to me?" I asked. "Am I going back to Jersey to sell newspapers on street corners?" I was only half joking.

"Don't worry," he said. "Dave Bing is gonna be the head coach. You're okay because I told them that they should keep you. So you'll be one of Bing's assistants."

I was fine with that. Bing had been a great player for the Pistons, and he was a smart guy. In fact, he later became the mayor of Detroit. But for the time being, bringing him onboard required some negotiations. In the meantime, while they were working through a contract with Bing, ownership came to me and asked me to be the interim head coach. It rocked me on my heels. Me? An NBA head coach? Even with an *interim* label it hardly seemed real.

A funny thing happened, though. The negotiations with Bing broke down, and I kept coaching the team game after game for the rest of the season. That was the good news. Any coach who has an interim tag attached to them is motivated to prove to ownership that they need to remove that word *interim* entirely and make him the *permanent* coach.

On December 4 Davidson came to me before the game and told me they were removing the interim tag. We were playing the Boston Celtics that night. Before the game, one the referees, Dick Bavetta, made some small talk with me. He was from New York, and I had known him forever. "Us guys from back East need to stick together," he said. "Yeah, we sure do," I said, happy to hear that.

Late in the game, we were up 3 points with seven seconds to go. The Celtics called a timeout to set up a play. We knew they were going to attempt a three-point play, not only because they were down by three, but also because they had three guys who could nail a three-pointer—Larry Bird, Chris Ford, and Dave Cowens. We were mainly concerned with Bird and Ford, and we had them defended. Cowens broke free at the top of the key and launched a three-pointer. The ball hit the rim and caromed to the left corner. M. L. Carr, the guy we had dealt to the Celtics the year before in the McAdoo trade, hustled after the ball and saved it from going out of bounds. He spun around, shuffling his feet to get set, and heaved the ball from the corner. It went in and tied the game, sending it into overtime, all while I was screaming at Bavetta, "He walked! He walked!" As I did, I was spinning my hands for the traveling sign. It was to no avail, and the Celtics ended up beating us 118–114.

Coaches never forget calls that cost them the game, and to this day, whenever I see Bavetta I kiddingly tell him, "Yeah, I guess us guys from back East really need to stick together."

Instead of what would have been euphoria, it was a downer after the game. That's when Davidson came into the locker room and announced to the team, "Fellas, tough loss. You played a great game. I just want you to know that we're naming Richie as the permanent coach the rest of the year." It was wonderful to hear him say that in front of the team, but I sure wish we could've coupled that announcement with a great win against the Celtics.

As it was, even with the loss, whatever small measure of euphoria I did feel was short-lived. Davidson and our new general manager, Jack McCloskey, decided they wanted to trade Lanier. From Davidson's point of view, he loved Lanier and wanted him to play for a contender. Conversely, the vibe I got from McCloskey was that he just didn't like Lanier, and that it was personal. Either way, the two of them felt this was a rebuilding situation, and they traded Lanier to Milwaukee for a first-round draft pick and an average young center named Kent Benson. That made us the youngest team in the NBA, and our one big veteran, Bob McAdoo, sat out the second half of the season with injuries. It became clear to me that the front office wanted us to lose to improve our draft pick. We had no chance. You're not going to win too many games when you trade away your superstar center, a future Hall of Famer. I knew there was no way we were going to win enough games for me to keep my job.

I was coaching as best as I could, working nonstop, and the guys took notice. These were young players, and they could see how hard I was getting after it. One day, as a group, they came into my office and said, "Coach, we're going to do our best in the next ten games so that you don't lose your job." It overwhelmed me, and it's something I'll never forget. Young or old, you just don't get that kind of over-the-top support in the NBA. It didn't work, though. They tried. I tried. But we didn't have the manpower and we kept losing. I coached seventy games that season, and only won twelve of them. I lost more games that one season than I did my entire eighteen years as a head coach in high school and college, when I had a combined 290-85 record. It was also the first time I ever had a losing record.

After the season, McCloskey called me into his office and told me what I expected to hear—that I wasn't going to be retained, which is a nice way of saying you're fired. I don't care who you are, it rattles you. You question yourself, especially when your firing comes after losing fifty-eight games and winning only twelve.

The next season, my replacement, Scotty Robertson, didn't fare much better—going 21-61. I didn't feel good about Scotty losing as badly as I did, but it did confirm to me that no matter how good of a coach you are, you still need the players. There is no substitute for having those horses.

I didn't have the horses. And now I didn't have a job.

5

Unfortunately, You Can Go Home Again

I t was the worst day of my life. The day after Labor Day, 1980.
First day of school. Not just any school. Public school in
Paterson, New Jersey's inner city. An eighth-grade teacher
at School No. 13. I just shook my head. It seemed as if in the
snap of a finger I went from coaching an NBA team to standing in a dank middle school hallway, waiting for barely teenage kids to arrive who were as unhappy to be there as I was. As
I looked up and down the hallway, I kept muttering to myself,
"How did I get here?"

I walked into my classroom and the realization struck me
like a two-by-four across the forehead. This was going to be
my nineteenth year teaching public school in the inner city.
But I had no choice. Instead of knocking at my door, the NDA
had shown me the door. And I had children to house and feed.

The students started filing in, as disinterested as I was.
Three belligerent girls, the kind who always seem to have an
argumentative attitude, sat in a row and promptly put their
feet on their desks. I wanted to say something, but I didn't have
enough ire. Then another kid walked in wearing this ridiculous plume hat. I'd seen enough. I walked over, snatched it off
his head and flung it aside.

"Coach, you're going to ruin my hat," he protested.

"I'm going to ruin you!" I barked, and I think the menacing tone in my voice said more than the words did. I wasn't in a good mood, certainly in no mood to be screwed with, and they instinctively knew it.

Eventually, my love for kids took over, and I knew they deserved my best. Something kicks in and you understand that you can change a life, perhaps even save a life, and before you realize it you're pouring yourself into trying to help.

Years later I was reminded of the impact you could have on kids by a college teammate of mine named Joe Clark. Joe and I played basketball together at Paterson State—now called William Paterson University. After graduating, Joe stayed in Paterson as a teacher. He later became the principal at Paterson East Side High School, which was notorious for its drugs and gang violence. Joe turned that school around. It was amazing what he did. In fact, they made a movie that told the story of the impact Joe had and what he did at that high school. It was called *Lean on Me*. Morgan Freeman played the role of Joe Clark.

Nobody was coming to me with a Hollywood contract, but I always knew I cared about kids and wanted to help. Others saw that too. Because of my reputation, the school system eventually gave me the special assignment of tutoring kids, mostly sick kids, often terminal, who couldn't make it to school. I said I wanted to help kids. And I did. But those kids helped me more than I helped them.

I'll never forget one girl named Mary, who was blind and had slight brain damage. Mary was fourteen. I'd go to her home five days a week, an hour each time, to teach her; in preparation I'd gone to the Passaic County School for the Blind to learn a little Braille. The first time I went to her home she was there with her mother and little sister, and they were watching a rerun of the television show *I Dream of Jeannie*. Her mother told me it was Mary's favorite show. I had learned some rudimentary skills in reading Braille; and we would do some Braille work together and then watch *I Dream of Jeannie*, and she started calling me Major, after the Larry Hagman character.

One day, when I walked in, Mary said, "What are we going to do today, Major? That's a very nice blue jacket you have on."

I was stunned. I looked down and it *was* a blue jacket!

"What color is my shirt?" I asked, my mouth dropping.

"I think it's pink."

She was right. I looked at her mother wide eyed. She looked at me with even wider eyes. And it was all because of Mary's eyes. She could see! I called the Board of Education to tell my friend Mike Mugno. They had her examined and found that indeed her eyesight had improved. I was ecstatic for her. When news of what happened spread through the Board of Education, they started calling me the Messiah, because only Jesus could perform such miracles—curing the blind. But I must say that I preferred my little friend calling me Major.

Sometimes—all too often, really—the health of these poor children went south. I was assigned to teach history and English—one hour a day, five days a week—to a teenage girl who was enrolled at Paterson Catholic High School but was too sick to go to school. I didn't know what her illness was. Nobody ever told me. It was a wonderful family, though, and she had a twin sister.

One day, her mother called to tell me that her daughter was too sick to be taught that day. More days went by, then a week, two weeks, three, four. When I called a month later, I was told she had been admitted into St. Joseph's Hospital in Paterson. I took it upon myself to visit her, bringing flowers and candy. But when I entered the room, I was taken aback. This beautiful 115-pound girl was an 80-pound shell of herself, gaunt and pale, her eyes hollow, telegraphing death. I saw her parents at a corner of the room, praying to a Virgin Mary statue. I burst out crying. Her father saw me and ushered me into the hallway. That's when I learned she had leukemia. She died a month later. All these years later, her memory haunts me, and I often wonder about the fate of her twin sister, kicking myself that I never bothered to stay in touch with the family.

I still wanted back in the NBA. Once you get that taste, you can't get it out of your mouth. Nor do you want to. But at the same time, being around those kids made me appreciate what I did have and to not even dare dwell on any self-pity.

There was another kid who really got to me. My friend Mugno was head of a program called Career Development. Kids would go to school for half a day and then go to work for half a day. I would tutor those kids in the mornings and then make sure they went to their jobs in the afternoons, checking in with their employers. I actually enjoyed it, and I got to see more of what it was like in the inner city. Still, it wasn't easy. I was to tutor one fourteen-year-old Puerto Rican girl who'd had a lover who was thirty-five. That was shocking enough. Even more so, though, was that he had gotten jealous of her one day and shot her in the back, paralyzing her. In a wheelchair now, she was extremely distraught and didn't want anybody to help her. I got that message the first time I arrived at her house and introduced myself to her parents. She was in her room, and I could hear her throwing something that *thwacked* against the door.

I opened it a crack, leaned in, and said, "I'd love to help you. I brought you flowers and candy. You've had a horrible tragedy. Please take these gifts."

That didn't just get me in, it got me through to her. I taught her for several months, and it became a huge success story. Passaic County had a school for children who needed wheelchairs, and I was able to get her in. In time she pulled her life together, graduated from high school, and got a job working as a receptionist.

As I mentioned, I believe those kids taught me more than I taught them. I learned the importance of honesty, because those kids could see right through you if you weren't honest with them, and you were through when that happened. Honesty, sincerity, understanding them and what they think about themselves and their lives, those were like keys that unlocked deeper meanings. I took those lessons into all walks of life. I'd like to believe, too, that reaching those less fortunate kids, and truly making an effort to understand them, helped me later to communicate with NBA players, many of whom came from similar backgrounds.

I don't mind saying that I'm proud of the fact that I was the only white guy they sent into those inner-city neighborhoods. Others tried, but they either couldn't handle it, or they were run out—or worse. One of my fellow teachers in Career Development was a white guy, about fifty years old. His first day on the job he was assigned to an area in Paterson called the Alabama Projects. It was one of the most dangerous places in the country, overrun with drug dealers and criminals, just a horrible place. Well, this fellow teacher, a really nice guy who just didn't know any better, got all dressed up for his first visit, putting on a suit. That was his first mistake. His second mistake was taking the elevator instead of the stairs, the latter of which you always do in the projects. When you get in an elevator and they get in behind you, you're trapped. Sure enough, they jumped him inside that elevator, stole his wallet and beat him badly. He got reassigned to a safer area.

Taking a cue from that incident, I met one kid from the Alabama Projects at a diner across the street from where he lived. I'd buy him lunch and teach him there. That made an impression, I'm sure. And if you care, and you really are trying to make a difference, word gets around, and there is an unspoken measure of respect and safety you're afforded.

But you couldn't always avoid going into those homes. Once, when I walked into a rundown apartment, cockroaches were all over the walls and scurrying in and out of the sink. The mother began cooking lunch, and she got a pot of soup going. Before it got too hot, I noticed the cockroaches crawling in and out of the pot, and she wasn't bothered by it at all. After I introduced myself, I told them I had a habit of sliding the table away from the wall and banging it a few times so the cockroaches wouldn't bother us while we studied. Then I'd sit in the middle of the room and teach the kid. It helped. But I also learned soon enough to bring a long flat stick with me, so that if any cockroaches got near the table while we were studying, I'd flatten 'em. Oh, and I also wised up soon enough to the danger of wearing pants with cuffs, because those cockroaches would hide in those cuffs and ride home with you, then they'd multiply and make your home theirs.

You never felt comfortable in those neighborhoods, no matter how much goodwill you had built. One morning at the projects, I was going into an apartment complex that had some big metal doors that served as a sort of gate. Four bad-looking dudes were sitting out front, looking hungover. My muscles tensed as I walked past them. Just when I got past the big metal doors and could feel myself exhale, I heard a loud *bang! bang!* I was sure it was gunshots. I whipped around, crouching in what I called my karate stance. The four guys busted out laughing. I realized that the wind had slammed the metal doors shut. I started laughing, too. The language of mutual laughter made me feel at ease, if not safe, and I went in.

It was early in 1982, and I was two years into working as a Career Development-Bedside Teacher. But typical of me, I always worked several jobs, which always included bartending. Two of my Jersey Guys, Hubie Brown and Mike Fratello, were coaching the Atlanta Hawks; Hubie as the head coach and Fratello as an assistant. They hired me to be a regional scout, which was perfect for me, and them. I was teaching in Paterson and bartending in the Meadowlands, which is where the New Jersey Nets played. I was also a half hour from Madison Square Garden, where the New York Knicks played. It took me an hour and ten minutes to get to Philadelphia, where the 76ers played. I was also a quick flight away from either Washington DC or Boston, where the Bullets and Celtics played. I could also scout all the college players in the region. Like a lifeline, it kept me tethered to the game. But when Hubie got fired from the Hawks on March 26, 1981, with only three games remaining in the season, I was back down to two jobs.

I was bartending one night when all of a sudden Hubie and Fratello walked in. I was surprised to see them but even more surprised to hear what Hubie had to say. "I just got the New York Knicks job, a four-year contract," he told me, "and we're going to bring you with us to be our second assistant."

I couldn't believe what I was hearing. As sad as that day in 1980 was, this was the opposite end of the spectrum. I was ecstatic. Just a great, great day! Not only was I going back to the NBA, I was going to the New York Knicks, the team I had grown up rooting for. We celebrated with a few cocktails, and Hubie and Mike left about midnight. They told me to come in the next morning and sign a contract. I couldn't wait to close and go home. The sun couldn't rise fast enough, but I had to stick it out until closing time, which was 3 a.m.

About two o'clock in the morning, an influx of people rolled in, most of them already drunk, which wasn't unusual because most of the other neighborhood bars closed at two. That hour between two and three was usually wild, the time of the night when we had the most problems. But just as those people in the bar that night were feeling no pain, neither was I. I was going back to the NBA and feeling euphoric.

It was a bitter cold September night, and around two-thirty this guy wearing a big coat walked in. He must have been six feet five. I was working the bar with three women and he walked right up, sat down, and ordered three beers. One of the women put three beers in front of him and he started drinking. What he didn't do was reach for his wallet.

She came over to me and said, "Richie, this guy hasn't put any money on the bar. I'm not sure what to do."

I walked down to where he was sitting. "Excuse me," I said, "but you know nothing's free here. You're going to have to pay for those beers."

He stood and looked at me, and I could see in his eyes that he was high. On what? I didn't know. But he was definitely high. Great, I thought, I'm going into New York in several hours to sign a contract with the New York Knicks. I don't need any problems. Not tonight. I turned to walk away, and just then he came across the bar top with his forearm and all three beer bottles went flying. Bottles crashed off the cash register, the mirror—everything went flying. Very calmly, as if nothing had happened, he walked down the bar toward the bathroom, with people scattering out of his way.

It was a Monday night, so we had no bouncers working. I wasn't taking any chances. I called the police and two cops came quickly. The problem was, they weren't very big guys—maybe about five feet ten. When he came out of the bathroom, the cops tried to grab him, but he swatted them away, sending them flying in different directions.

Anticipating that things might not go as planned, I'd given a few of the patrons I knew fifth bottles of booze, just in case. I chose fifth bottles because they had handles on them that would allow whoever was holding them to grab the bottle easily and swing it like a weapon. No sooner had the cops gone flying when several of those guys jumped him and started pounding him with those bottles. With the help of the cops, they finally got him cuffed and out of there.

I got out of there, too. I got home, cleaned up, and got to the Knicks' office at eight, an hour before most of the workers arrived. Hubie and Mike got there at ten, and they heard I'd been waiting for two hours.

"Why'd you get here so early?" Hubie asked.

"I'm just anxious to sign my contract," I said.

It was a two-year contract. But I didn't care if it was two months, two weeks, or two days. I was back in the NBA.

6

From the Garden State to Madison Square Garden

I t was 1982 and I was happy to be with my boys again, and even happier to be back in the NBA, and especially happy to be at Madison Square Garden with the New York Knicks. Imagine that, the Jersey Guys were now in New York, and I was on a Knicks staff with my pals Hubie Brown and Mike Fratello. I couldn't believe my good fortune.

It didn't surprise me that Hubie was well on his way to becoming a great NBA coach. He was meticulous in his detail in all facets of the game, and he was more organized than crime. Because of the way Hubie coached, I believe nobody played harder than those Knicks teams in the 1980's. Hubie's philosophy was to play ten guys every night. His thinking was that if you didn't play forty to forty-five minutes—if you instead played about thirty minutes—nobody would get tired, and perhaps even more importantly, everybody would play defense.

As with all great coaches, Hubie was goal oriented and, not surprisingly, he was specific with the goals he wanted us to achieve. How many times would we force a turnover? How many steals would we get? How many shots would we block? How many shots would we challenge without fouling? Because of that, those Knicks teams were always one of the top five defensive teams in the league. As an assistant, and as a guy whose specialty was defense, I kept a running tally of our important statistics, especially those related to those specific goals Hubie wanted us to meet.

For whatever reason, though, we struggled defending against the fast break. One game in particular, Hubie was really upset that the opposing team was running us hard, and we weren't getting back on the defensive end of the court in time. He called timeout, but he wouldn't let the guys sit. When Hubie did that, he was sending a message that he thought the guys weren't hustling.

"Richie," he said, turning to me, "how many fast breaks do they have against us?"

I looked at my stat sheet. "They're 8 for 10 on the break," I said.

"How many offensive rebounds do we have, Richie?"

"We have three."

Hubie pointed at one end of the court, where they were running on us, and said, "Well, you guys are obviously not *here*, because they're 8 for 10 on the fast break." Then he pointed to the other end of the court where we were on offense, where we only had three offensive rebounds, and he said, "You're not *there* either. So if you're not *here* and you're not *there*, then where the hell are you!?" The guys on the bench started laughing hysterically. But Hubie wasn't amused. His message worked, though, and the guys started hustling better.

Needless to say, Hubie was a taskmaster, and in that era he could get away with his hard-nosed style of coaching. He won the ABA Championship in 1975 and was two-time NBA Coach of the Year. Plus, in 2005 he was inducted into the Naismith Memorial Basketball Hall of Fame. I learned a lot from Hubie, but boy he was tough—both on players and also on his coaches. You always ran a little scared with Hubie. Right after I got to the Knicks in 1982, I was in San Diego, back when the Clippers' franchise still played there. I was doing advance scouting during the preseason when Mike Fratello called.

"You're in Utah, right?" he said.

"No, Mike. I'm not in Utah. I'm in San Diego."

"San Diego? Uh-oh, Richie. Hubie thinks you're in Utah. He's going to be pissed. He thinks you're in Utah and he wants you to get some additional information on Bernard King."

I knew we were interested in trading for Bernard King, a Brooklyn kid who at the time was with the Golden State Warriors, who were scheduled to be in Salt Lake City to play the Jazz. And, according to Hubie, I was scheduled to be there, too. It was four o'clock in the afternoon. I hung up the phone, made a quick call, and learned there was a five o'clock flight to Salt Lake City. I threw my stuff into my little carry-on suitcase, ran downstairs, flagged a cabbie and told him, "Here's a hundred bucks! Just get me to the airport any way you can!"

It was a wild ride. He was taking shortcuts everywhere—going through driveways, back alleys, on sidewalks—but I was more nervous about incurring the wrath of Hubie Brown.

I got to the airport ten minutes before the flight's departure. I looked like O. J. Simpson in those old Hertz commercials running through an airport. This was back before security and checkpoints, and I ran straight to the gate, right onto the plane, and straight to the restroom, shutting the door and breathing hard. After they shut the door, backed away from the gate, and took off, I came out. A flight attendant approached me. "Excuse me, sir," she said. "I know you were in a hurry, but you didn't give us your ticket."

"I know," I said. "Here's my credit card. I'm sorry, I don't have a ticket. I didn't have time to buy one. It was an emergency situation. I don't care how much you charge me for this flight—and take fifty dollars as a tip—I just have to get there."

She was nice about it. "We'll take care of it when we land," she said.

After we landed and I paid whatever they were asking for the airline ticket, I jumped into another cab, handed the guy a fifty-dollar bill and said, "I don't care what you do, just please get me to the arena as quick as you can."

I reached my seat at the Salt Palace just as the opening tip-off was going up. Hubie never knew anything different. Oh, and we did wind up trading Micheal Ray Richardson and a 1984 fifth-round draft pick to the Warriors for Bernard King, which was probably the greatest trade the Knicks have ever made. Bernard became a phenomenal scoring machine for us. He could take over a game and explode with a flurry of points. Just unstoppable.

Before knee injuries ravaged King and his career, he had some of the NBA's all-time greatest seasons, the best of which was the 1984–85 season, when he averaged 32.9 points per game, leading the league. But it was the year before, when we played the Boston Celtics in the Eastern Conference Semifinals that I'll most remember. Bernard King and Larry Bird were exchanging baskets like heavyweight fighters exchanging punches. Back and forth it went—two great players elevating their games, trying to outdo each other. King averaged 29.1 points that series and Bird 30.4 points. In Games Four and Six at Madison Square Garden, King scored 43 and 44 points, respectively. But it was Bird's 39 points at the Boston Garden in Game Seven that clinched the series for the Celtics, en route to beating the Los Angeles Lakers in the NBA Finals.

You can appreciate, then, why it was so important for me to be in Utah, scouting Bernard King before we decided to trade for him, and why I went to such insane lengths to ensure that I got there in time to see him play a preseason game. It's those little things, like getting a solid scouting report on a player you're interested in, that can lead to big results. It's why, of course, Hubie Brown was such a hard-ass stickler for those things.

One of the scouts on our staff whom I worked closely with was Dick McGuire. Dick had done everything in basketball— and I do mean *everything*. He was an All-Star point guard, a head coach, a scout, and eventually, like Hubie, an inductee into the Naismith Memorial Basketball Hall of Fame. But through all the things he had experienced, McGuire never experienced anybody quite like Hubie Brown.

Hubie would have us meet for breakfast every morning at seven thirty. But we didn't eat much. Instead, we'd go over the schedule for the day—the practices, the breakdowns, what we were trying to accomplish. And it was intense. Hubie challenged you; kept you on your toes. One morning, McGuire and one of our other scouts, Fuzzy Levane, were sitting at another table. They weren't required to sit in on our meetings, but I figured I'd invite them. "Hey guys, we're discussing practice," I said. "Why don't you come over and join us?"

McGuire looked at me as if I'd just landed from outer space. "I'm not joining that table," he said. "Even the eggs are nervous over there."

McGuire was a tremendous talent evaluator. He was also blunt. Since I was involved with the college draft and all the advance scouting, I'd get McGuire's reports, and if he said, "They can't play," then that was it. As far as McGuire was concerned, that particular guy couldn't play in the NBA, and nothing more needed to be said.

But then we got new ownership, and they wanted to be a little more involved. A former great Knicks player, Dave DeBusschere, was now our general manager, and one day he called McGuire into his office. "Dick, this is not questioning your talent evaluating. We know how good you are," he said. "But we have new ownership and you just can't write on the report, 'Can't play.' They're going to want more information than that. So could you be a little more specific?"

About a week later, DeBusschere called me over.

"Richie, I want you to see this," he said. "I told Dick he had to say a little bit more about each player. Look at what he put in his report."

I looked at the scouting report and it read: "Can't play. In this league."

My two-year contract that began in 1982 stretched into four years, and I enjoyed every minute of it. Because I was involved with the college draft, guys were always telling me to keep an eye on this player or that player. But one time when I was in Los Angeles, a college player came up to me at a Lakers game and told me to keep an eye on *him*. "Excuse me, coach," the college kid said, introducing himself, "I know you're a coach with the Knicks. I play for UCLA, and I just want to tell you that I'm going to be a great pro player."

I noticed that this kid was a college sophomore—a *sophomore*. But he reiterated that he was going to be an NBA player and added, "Before it's over I'm going to be tremendous in the NBA."

Him saying that really didn't bother me. I don't mind guys with great confidence, who believe in themselves. I think it's terrific. What bothered me was that this kid was really slight; just a very, very skinny kid.

"I'll keep watching you," I said. "But you've gotta hit the weights because this league is very physical. You're gonna find yourself matched up with guys who have a lot of size and strength on you. They're gonna post you up and it's gonna be really tough."

"I'll work on the weights a little bit," he said. "But it really doesn't matter because no one can guard me and no one shoots the ball as quickly as I do."

"Okay, fine," I said. "I'll be watching."

And I did watch. I watched this skinny kid get drafted eleventh overall by the Indiana Pacers in the 1987 NBA Draft, seven picks ahead of us (we selected Mark Jackson). I watched him become a five-time All-Star. I watched him make more than $104 million in his career. And in 2012, I watched Reggie Miller get inducted into the Naismith Memorial Basketball Hall of Fame.

It just goes to show that judging talent is not an exact science, and you never know where that talent is going to come from. At the same time, you have to be willing to go anywhere to find that talent. On Friday nights, there was a basketball league in Spanish Harlem. It was formed to keep guys off the streets, keep them away from the drugs, and hopefully keep them out of trouble. A couple of our Knicks players—Ray Williams and Rory Sparrow—had played there, which got Hubie's attention.

"You and Bobby go up there and check out some of the talent," he told me one day, speaking about Bob Hill, who in 1985 had become one of our assistant coaches.

The league was called Midnight Basketball, and they actually did play at midnight—from midnight to about three in the morning. When Hill came to pick me up he was wearing a shiny satin silver warm-up suit.

"Bobby," I said, incredulous. "You're not wearing *that*, are you?"

"Yeah, I'm wearing *that*," he said. "Why?"

"Bobby, we're going to Spanish Harlem. Midnight. Midnight to three in the morning. Friday night. Um, I wouldn't wear that outfit. We're liable to get mugged. Some guy'll take that outfit from you and get married in it."

He started laughing. "I'm not worried about it," he said.

"Okay," I said. "You're six feet five. I just hope you're as tough as you think you are."

We got to Spanish Harlem and found a parking spot on the street about three blocks from the gym. It was a hot summer night and everybody was out, and everybody was drinking. They were hanging out on porches, on the corners, in the streets, and you could tell it was all bad.

"Man, Bobby," I said, as we started walking toward the gym, "I wish you hadn't worn that outfit 'cause we gotta walk about three blocks to the gym, and it doesn't look good."

Guys started whistling from all corners of the streets, and before I knew it there were five guys behind us, following from about twenty feet, closing in. "Uh-oh," I said, "I think we're going to have some problems here, buddy." I felt my shoulders tense, and from the corner of my eye I could see Bobby's face tighten. Thankfully we got close enough to the gym, where there were some cops standing around, and nothing happened. After we told the cops who we were, they escorted us in. The gym was packed and loud. Not only was the basketball good, the fans were knowledgeable. When they recognized Hill and me, they were shouting at us what they thought the Knicks needed.

I found one of the cops when we were ready to leave and asked him to walk us back to our car. "Why, are you worried?" he asked.

"Believe me," I said, "I'm worried."

When we got the three blocks back to the car it was stripped. The rims and tires were gone, as well as anything else that could be taken off it.

"Welcome to New York City," the cop said. "This ain't Kansas."

He was nice enough to give us a lift to Madison Square Garden, where we stayed at a hotel that night and headed home the next day.

As edgy as that night was, it wasn't the most harrowing experience I had during my time with the Knicks. No, the most harrowing experience happened *inside* Madison Square Garden. We'd been on the road for a while, long enough for the Ringling Bros. and Barnum & Bailey Circus to enjoy a run of performances at the Garden. When we came back for our first home game in a while, Mike Fratello and I were walking down a hallway where a bunch of chimpanzees were in cages, lined up along the side of a wall. As we walked by they started spitting on us.

"I'm not coming this way again," I told Fratello. "Not with these nice suits we're wearing." After the game, I reminded Fratello of the chimps. "I don't want to walk past them again and let them spit on us."

"Don't worry," he said. "I know a shortcut to our office."

I followed him, going a route I'd never taken before. That's Madison Square Garden. It's so huge there are places you can get lost through all the maze of hallways; places you didn't even know existed. As I'm following Fratello—and we were still about fifty yards from our office—we went through a door I'd never gone through before. When it shut behind us it locked. That's when I saw something that still makes my heart race just thinking about it—cages and cages of lions and tigers. It was late, and they had been sleeping. But as soon as we walked in they roused to attention. I could see their cat eyes contracting and focusing on us. The next thing I knew their giant paws were trying to claw at us through the bars on their cages as I heard the rumbling of growls. The hallway was so tight that Fratello and I literally had our backs against the wall, inching our way along about thirty yards to the next door.

"Nice shortcut," I told Fratello after we finally got out of there.

Playing in New York City is unlike any other place in the world. I don't believe you'll find more passionate fans anywhere else. When you're winning, you're gold. But if you're losing, New York fans have no problem letting you know—on subways, on the streets, in restaurants. It can get brutal. When we started the 1982 season 0-7, we really heard it. Everywhere we turned, it was, "You guys suck!"

We coaches used to go to the Carnegie Deli after home games. It was a popular restaurant that always had a line of people waiting to get in. The owner, Freddie Klein, was a huge Knicks fan, so we never had to wait in line to get in. After our sixth-straight loss—to the New Jersey Nets, no less—we went in through the back door, with Freddie providing us our usual table. Right after we sat down, a group of fans noticed us and approached our table, and I thought, "Oh boy, we're really going to hear it now." To my surprise they stood there and applauded us. It was as if we were getting a standing ovation.

"You guys covered the spread every single game," one of them said.

On one hand I was relieved. On the other hand . . .

I was never a gambler. I certainly never bet on basketball. I tried betting on football a few times, and I lost every time. I got tired of losing money, plus I could never just enjoy the game, so I quit gambling after those few forays. But if you're in professional sports you're aware that gambling goes on. It's scary sometimes to see just how good the oddsmakers are. You could put a bunch of coaches together and they couldn't come close to the accuracy of those guys in Las Vegas. And, as coaches, we know the game, we know the players, we know the injuries, we know the schemes, we know the philosophies.

We know everything. But somehow the Vegas guys always know more.

And as weird as it was to get applauded after losing our first six games to start the 1982–83 season, I remember once getting booed at Madison Square Garden after Ernie Grunfeld hit a three-pointer for us with about fifty seconds left in a game, putting us up by 15 points. As the boos rained down, I couldn't figure out why. "I don't know what's going on," I told Ernie afterward, "but if I were you, I'd go out the back exit."

A few days later I was scouting some college teams in the Meadowlands and I ran into a friend of mine named Danny, who was a bookie.

"Danny, how ya doin'?" I asked.

Danny, an Italian guy who spoke broken English, looked at me and said, "Richie, that sum-a-bitch Ernie Grun-a-feld, he hitta the three. I lost twenty G."

It boggles my mind—losing $20,000 on a regular-season basketball game. There are times when I tell myself that I don't even want to know what I don't know. I'd rather be ignorant to that stuff. But I will say this: there were times when I scouted college games and I knew, I just *knew*, there was point-shaving going on.

The 1980s were a great time to be in the NBA, to see the growth of the league and the emergence of players like Magic Johnson and Larry Bird. What I learned from guys like that was you never wanted great players to come off a bad game with you next on the schedule, because the great ones always have a comeback game after a bad one. Bird was certainly that way. I remember once he was coming to the Garden after an off night and it had me worried. When I got to the Garden early, I saw that Bird was already there. He had paid the ball boy to come early with him so he could work on his shot. I knew we were in trouble.

Sure enough, seconds into the game, Bird came down and launched a three-point shot from a few feet behind the line. *Swish!* Hubie called to our guys, "That's all right! You don't have to pick him up that far out!" Hubie reasoned that from that distance it was a low-percentage shot, so let Bird have at it.

A few plays later, Bird came down, caught the ball at least five feet behind the three-point line. Sitting on the bench we all thought: no way. He launched it again and *swish!* it hit nothing but net. As Bird backpedaled on defense, he turned to Hubie and with a nod of his head said, "Hey Hubie, is that deep enough?"

That was Bird, one of the toughest, most competitive players I ever saw. I recall one year at the All-Star Game he came into the locker room before the Three-Point Shooting Contest and said, "I don't know who's gonna come in second, but I'm winning this." And he did. I had a casual conversation with him once, and he said it always aggravated him whenever they put a white guy on him to defend him, that it was a sign of disrespect. "If they put a white guy on me, they have no chance," he said. I don't think he was joking.

Those were some great years—four fabulous years—and there were many times I had to pinch myself: not only was I back in the NBA, but it looked like this time I was sticking. Little did I know, though, that my time with the Knicks was coming to an end.

7

From the Big Apple to Big D

One thing I didn't have with the New York Knicks that I had with my buddy Dick Vitale when we were with the Detroit Pistons was the stature of being the top assistant coach, or what we call the first assistant. I missed that. One thing I didn't miss, however, was a phone call that came out of the blue in the summer of 1986. It was Dick Motta, the Dallas Mavericks' head coach. He wanted me to interview to be his top assistant coach—his *first* assistant.

"I hate defense," Motta said.

"I love defense," I told him, although he already knew that.

By now I had gained a reputation around the NBA for putting together very effective defensive schemes. Defense isn't sexy and it isn't what most coaches enjoy, but I had a passion for it and there was the added bonus that it kept me in the league. Now it looked as if it might get me what you would call a promotion.

Aside from being well connected as one of the Jersey Guys, another benefit of being from the New Jersey–New York– Pennsylvania area is that all of us coaches who cut our teeth there were indoctrinated into a defensive philosophy and mindset by Bobby Knight, going back to when Knight was the head coach at Army in West Point, New York. Some really great defensive minds emerged from that tristate area—guys like

Hubie Brown; Rollie Massimino; Al LoBalbo, the legendary coach and defensive genius from Fairleigh Dickinson University; and Rick Pitino, who is one of the best coaches ever at implementing a press defense.

I flew to Dallas when the Mavericks were conducting some off-season summer practices in the form of two daily sessions—an hour and a half in the morning and an hour and a half in the afternoon.

"Jump in anytime you see something or you want to make any additional comments," Motta said.

So I did.

Two of the front-office executives, Rick Sund and Norm Sonju, were at the morning session. Afterward, Motta asked for my input and then told me to run the entire afternoon practice. With Motta, Sund, and Sonju watching, I ran the practice from start to finish. Naturally, I emphasized defense, if only so they could see my approach. I could tell Motta was impressed. A little later, Sund called and offered me the job.

I was going from the Big Apple to Big D.

The first game of the season saw us at home playing the Utah Jazz. I was ready. Pregame in the locker room I drew up ten defensive fundamentals on the board. Motta walked in and stared at it.

"What's this?" he asked.

"It's the ten defensive keys to winning the game," I said.

"Good luck," he said with a slight smirk. "They're never going to remember all that. Take all that off and put three on there."

"Three!?" I said. "Dick, c'mon, gimme five."

"Okay, five. But only five."

With those five defensive schemes we held the Jazz to 77 points, while we scored 103 points in the victory. It was an impressive beatdown. In fact, the Jazz shot a Reunion Arena record low 31 percent. The next day, the headline in the sports section read: "Richie D."

You can practice and practice and practice, but that game and headline earned me respect with the players. They believed in my philosophy and could see that the system I was implementing worked. It worked throughout the season, in fact, with that team winning a franchise-record fifty-five regular-season games.

There were adjustments, though.

I was a Jersey guy entering a completely different environment. There is no place like Texas. It has a culture and a dialect all its own. It's hard to find any group of people in the country who talk faster than Jersey guys or slower than Texans. When I first arrived and went to see my new office, I was told, "Your office is over there and your secretary is Pie-at." Pie-at? I'd never heard of a name like that before. Must be a Texas name, I thought. When I went over to introduce myself to my secretary, I noticed a nameplate on her desk that read: P-A-T. Inside, I laughed. In Texas it's Pie-at, two syllables. In Jersey it's just Pat. Of course, with a last name like Adubato, who was I to say anything? My whole time there, the owner, Don Carter, and his family always called me "Coach Richie." They never seemed to understand me, or I them. I had my own TV and radio shows for a while, and they would say, "Coach, that sounds right, but can you say it a little slower." I'd say it twice as fast and then smile and say, "That sounds right to me." The entire time I spent in Dallas, that Texas drawl never even dented my Jersey accent. I don't know if that's a good thing or a bad thing. It just is what it is.

I did fall in love with Dallas, and I'd like to think the feeling was mutual. That first season was gold. The year before, the Mavericks were twenty-first in the NBA in points allowed. But in my first season as Dick Motta's top assistant, as his defensive specialist, we went 55-27 and jumped seven spots in the league in points allowed. Motta was a great guy to work with. We meshed well. He handled the offense, I handled the defense, and we won—a lot. That helps with any relationship in coaching.

As is the case with me, Motta could be a bit of a character. Back then, and even now, there could be some whacky half-

time entertainment at NBA games. We were to play the Portland Trail Blazers one night, and the scheduled halftime show
was a basket-shooting monkey riding on the back of a tiger.
Who thinks of such things? Before the game, I was in the locker
room, doing what I always did, which was write our defensive schemes on the board, when the door flew open and there
Dick stood with the tiger on a leash. I retreated, running into
the bathroom, frantically looking for a way out or someplace
where I could hide. Guys were screaming, jumping onto anything they could find, scrambling to get out of the way. Motta
paraded the tiger around the locker room, this devious smile
smeared across his face, and said before he left, "If we're not
winning at halftime, this guy is going to give you a motivational speech."

We were winning at halftime, thank goodness.

But there were some of Motta's antics that came back to
haunt him—and us as a team. I found that out in the first
round of the playoffs that season. Our fifty-five-win team finished second in the Western Conference to the powerhouse
Los Angeles Lakers. Still a relatively new franchise—the Mavericks were only in their seventh year of existence—we were
well stocked with star players, such as Mark Aguirre, Rolando
Blackman, Derek Harper, Sam Perkins, and an up-and-coming
rookie named Roy Tarpley. In the first round of the playoffs,
we were pitted against the Seattle SuperSonics—a team that
finished 39-43. We were expected to roll over them, especially
considering we beat them all five times by an average of 18.6
points in our five regular-season games against them.

Sure enough, in the first game of the five-game series we
exploded for 151 points, winning easily. In Game Two, they
hung tough with us, playing us closer than they had all season.
It was a back-and-forth game and it went down to the wire.
Seattle guard Dale Ellis hit a baseline jumper with 1:30 left to
tie the score at 110–110. He then missed a jumper with five seconds left, but Seattle got another chance at us when Harper
turned the ball over on an inbounds play. It was a freak call.

The normal progression in a situation like that was we'd set up a play, inbound the ball, and get a shot off to get the victory. But when Harper inbounded the ball, official Jack Madden blew his whistle. On an inbound pass you have to establish your pivot foot and not move. Madden claimed Harper moved his foot. I can't say that I saw it happen, but what I can say is that I'd never seen that called before, and certainly not in that kind of end-of-game situation in the playoffs.

Instead of being tied with the ball and five seconds to go, Seattle now had the ball. They called a timeout, set up a play, and got the ball to Ellis, who dribbled toward the right corner where three of our guys boxed him in. As he jumped to launch a shot, or maybe it was a pass, Perkins hit him and Ellis went sprawling. Once again, Madden blew his whistle. This time he raised two fingers, signaling two foul shots for Ellis. With our Reunion Arena fans going berserk behind the basket, Ellis calmly sank both free throws and we lost, 112–110. It was a stunning turn of events. I looked at Madden as he walked off the court, shaking my head, wondering why in the heck he had made that call against Harper, giving the SuperSonics the ball.

Turns out, both Madden and Ellis had it in for Motta—big time.

In his first three seasons in the league, Ellis rotted on the Mavericks' bench before Motta, who evidently told him he'd never be a two-guard in the NBA, traded him to Seattle before that 1986–87 season. Ellis promptly finished third in the NBA in scoring among all guards—behind Michael Jordan and Clyde Drexler. After the game, Ellis didn't hold back any of his venom. "I feel I was treated wrongly by Motta," he told reporters. "This was my opportunity to slap him and slap him hard. That's what I did with my free throws. It's the happiest day of my life. It's a moment I had dreamed about."

And then there was Madden, who also had a bit of history with Motta. Apparently there was an incident before I got to Dallas when Motta was unhappy with Madden's officiating. After what he thought was a bad call, the ball came rolling over to the Mavericks' bench. Motta picked it up and spit on it—a real gob. It's one thing to bring a live tiger into a locker room— something I'm sure Dick knew he had under control. It's quite another thing to hock up a loogie on a basketball and hand it to an unaware referee. When he came over to get the ball, Motta had his hand underneath the ball and turned it over so that Madden put his hand right on that gross mess.

Was the call in that playoff game retribution? I still wonder. Madden was a great official, but I'd never seen a call like that one against Harper on an inbound pass with a playoff game on the line. What was certain, though, is that Dale Ellis was out to get Dick Motta—and he did.

Making matters worse was that the next two games were in Seattle and not at the normal venue, the Seattle Center Coliseum, which for some reason wasn't available. Instead, we played at the University of Washington's Hec Edmundson Pavilion, which was smaller and more intimate—well, at least it was for Seattle fans. For us, it felt like a rabid, raucous crowd was right on top of us.

After blowing out Seattle in Game One and losing such a heartbreaker in Game Two, we lost Game Three, 117–107, and were eliminated in a Game Four rout, 124–98.

That night, Motta and his wife and I went to a restaurant overlooking Puget Sound and just sat there for about two hours, saying nothing. No words. No eye contact. Just empty stares off into space. I think we wanted to jump into Puget Sound and drown ourselves. We were that devastated.

Another shock came a few weeks later, when Motta, the only head coach the Mavericks had ever known, abruptly resigned. I'd caught wind he was thinking of quitting and took Dick to lunch. I begged him to stay. I thought I had changed his mind, but he called a news conference and announced he was leaving. I was floored. The owner loved him. The players loved him. We just had a record-setting year. Dick gave neither the media nor me an explanation. I knew Motta and Mark Aguirre were butting heads, and at the same time, ownership really liked Aguirre, and I guessed maybe that was it. But it was just that—a guess. The reality is that on May 20, 1987, I watched as Motta told the assembled press corps, "I'm outta here." And so he was.

It would be almost three years before Dick would return to the NBA, becoming the head coach of the Sacramento Kings on January 4, 1990, when he replaced Jerry Reynolds. I could not afford such a luxury, nor did I want time off. I needed a job, and all I could think of was: Here we go again. Will I be going back to Paterson, New Jersey, to teach inner-city kids? My fears were allayed when Dallas hired John MacLeod, who'd had a lot of success during fourteen seasons with the Phoenix Suns, and thankfully, he retained me. MacLeod also brought in Garfield Heard and Clifford Ray as the other assistant coaches. I was relieved. I'd come to love Dallas, and I really loved the team we had.

Under MacLeod we almost had an identical regular-season record to the one we had in Motta's last season—winning fifty-three games, two less than we had the year before. The difference, though, is that we won the first two rounds of the playoffs—against the Houston Rockets (3–1) and Denver Nuggets (4–2)—before losing to the Los Angeles Lakers juggernaut in a hotly battled series that went the full seven games. The Lakers won the first two in Los Angeles. We won the next two in Dallas. They won the fifth game at home, we won the sixth at our place, and they closed us out at their place in Game Seven, 117–102. It was one of the greatest seven-game playoff series I'd ever been involved in—or seen. There were a lot of stars on that Lakers team—Kareem Abdul-Jabbar, James Worthy, Byron Scott, A. C. Green, Michael Cooper, Mychal Thompson, and Kurt Rambis. But in my mind, the guy who made that team go was Magic Johnson. You just couldn't matchup against Magic because he could play all five positions. As it was, that Lakers team went on to beat the Detroit Pistons in the NBA Finals, in a series that also went seven games.

As for us, I knew we were getting better, and it was a breakout year for Roy Tarpley, a kid I liked a lot and had gotten close to. Tarpley was a rebounding monster and terrific defender, and he won the NBA's Sixth Man Award that season. I had a lot of hope for the following season, but we had a rash of injuries that we could never seem to overcome. Our 1988–89 team finished 38-44, which was a huge letdown. There were criticisms of MacLeod: that he had inherited a great team from Motta, and that the reason we won fifty-three games and went so far in the playoffs was because of the momentum from what Dick had built. So, notwithstanding the injuries, going six games under .500 in his second season didn't endear MacLeod to the critics.

When we started the 1989–90 season with a 5-6 record—with that sixth loss coming in an embarrassing 47-point loss to Seattle—I knew it was bad. The media noted that it was the worst home loss ever at Reunion Arena and the second-worst loss in franchise history. You could argue that the franchise wasn't even a decade old so there wasn't a lot of franchise history to draw from, but that was a losing argument. We had other problems, too. Six games into the season, Tarpley, who had already been suspended once for drug problems, was suspended indefinitely following his arrest for driving while intoxicated.

We were losing, and John MacLeod was losing the team. Only eleven games into the season they called him in and, inexplicably, they fired him.

8

Back in the Saddle Again

I didn't have to wait long to learn of my fate after the Dallas Mavericks fired John MacLeod only eleven games into the 1989–90 season. As was the case when the Detroit Pistons fired my buddy Dick Vitale, I was named the interim head coach. It's the old double-edged sword. You're a head coach, and a head coach in the NBA no less, but you have that *interim* title attached to it like a ball and chain. I knew the drill. I also knew it was an opportunity, one that I was determined to make the most of.

After my introductory news conference, a writer from the *Dallas Morning News* named Mitch Lawrence approached me. "Richie," he said, "I've gotta tell you something. I'm from New Jersey."

"Oh really. Where?"

"From Montclair," he said. "And you were the best bartender I ever met."

A smile and a look of shock spread across my face. "You're kidding," I said, studying him now to see if I could recognize the face. I couldn't.

"I'm not kidding," Mitch said. "My buddies and I used to come into Tierney's all the time."

"And I was the best bartender you ever met?"

Now it was Mitch's turn to smile. "Number one," he said,

"you never charged us. And two, we were underage and you never checked our IDs. So that makes you the greatest bartender I've ever known."

Now we were both smiling.

From that day forward, I always had a great working relationship with Mitch, which is important for an NBA coach, and especially so for a journalist. Mitch was and is a pro, a terrific NBA writer and reporter. I trusted him to be fair and do right by me. At the same time, I'd also like to think that all those free drinks all those years ago had built up a little bit of goodwill and equity with him.

Being an NBA head coach—even an interim head coach— brings a certain level of prestige. It gains you access to people and places normally not afforded you. Not that I sought those things. Usually they came to me. One guy I crossed paths with was George W. Bush, who at the time was part of the Texas Rangers' ownership group. His political career hadn't really started yet, though his dad was president of the United States. We were chatting one day and he told me he always wanted to meet Dick Vitale. So I arranged for a lunch date—just the three of us. The thing about Vitale is that, if you ever spend time with him, you better be prepared for a gift package—or packages—to arrive. The other thing about Vitale is that his gifts are Dick Vitale basketballs, Dick Vitale T-shirts, Dick Vitale books . . . you get the idea. He will bombard you, almost nonstop.

Two weeks after our lunch date, I ran into George W. again, this time at an athletic club we both belonged to. "Hey Richie, thanks for setting up that lunch with Dick. I really enjoyed it," he said with an air of cockiness that was typical of the vibe he gave off. "But can you pass something along to him?" "What's that?" I asked. "Please tell Dick that one book is enough," he said.

The other thing about being an NBA head coach is that it seems as though everyone you've ever known in your past shows up, and they've all been your best friend—and they all want tickets. But there was one odd thing that happened when I ran into an old Jersey friend named Joe Pistone, whom I hadn't seen in about twenty years. Joe and I played ball together at Paterson State, and like me, he became a school teacher in Paterson. Then I lost track of him.

As I was walking into the locker room one night, at halftime of a home game, I happened to look up at the balcony, and I saw Joe sitting there. I recognized him right away, even though he had lost most of his hair. I instinctively waved at him and he somewhat hesitantly waved back.

"Joe!" I yelled. "Come down after the game!"

After the game, he came down and told me that he had stayed in touch with a mutual friend, a guy named Jackie, and that he was living nearby.

"Why didn't you call and tell me?" I said. "I can leave you tickets."

"I didn't want to bother you," he said.

"Please, it's no bother. Anytime you want I can leave you tickets. Hey, why don't we get together for lunch? What's your number? I'll give you a call."

"No, no," he said. "I'll give you a call."

I gave him my number, but after several days of not hearing from him, I called our mutual friend, Jackie.

"Jackie," I said, "I ran into Joe Pistone the other day at our game. I hadn't seen him in ages. I told him to give me a call and we'll grab lunch, but I haven't heard from him."

Jackie paused. "Richie, did you ever see the movie *Donnie Brasco*?"

"Yeah, I saw it. Great movie."

"That's Joe. That's Joe's life. Donnie Brasco is Joe Pistone."

"You're kidding? Donnie Brasco is Joe Pistone?" I repeated, as if I were trying to convince myself of the connection. "The guy we played ball with at Paterson?"

"Same guy," he replied.

Evidently, Joe had become an FBI agent who infiltrated the mafia, leading to dozens of arrests while simultaneously putting his life in perpetual danger. The movie was based on Joe's life as an undercover FBI agent, with Johnny Depp playing the role of Joe.

"He's been in witness protection for a number of years," Jackie said.

I never saw Joe again. Years later, we loosely touched base and talked about getting together in New Jersey, but once again nothing ever became of it. To be honest, I'm glad it didn't. I admired Joe for what he did, but how could I sit and have lunch with him and feel relaxed? I'd always be looking over my shoulder. I felt for Joe in that regard. It must be miserable. If I was worried about looking over my shoulder just for lunch, imagine what it must be like 24/7.

Another famous person I got to know was the country singer Charley Pride, who was a big NBA and Mavericks fan. Once, when we had a preseason game against the Phoenix Suns, we were to fly to Phoenix and then bus a few hours to an Indian reservation.

"Why don't you take my private plane," Charley offered. "This way you can fly to an airport near the reservation and then fly home right afterward."

"Great," I said, knowing it would save us a lot of time and effort.

When we got to his plane, I noticed it was a prop plane. I'm not a fan of prop planes, but I didn't want to say anything that might scare the players. We flew to Arizona without a problem. But on the way back, after about an hour in the air, the prop on the right side of the plane went dead. The players were turning all different shades of color; their panic was palpable. Meanwhile, they had migrated to the left side of the plane, staring at the working prop, which started to throw the plane off its ballast. The pilot came on and told us to get back in our seats, and that everything was okay. "Don't worry," he said, "because even if the prop on the left side stops, we can glide in."

We made an emergency landing in Tucson and had to stay in a hotel overnight while they repaired the prop. The next day the players refused to fly back in the prop plane, so we had to take a commercial flight back to Dallas.

Charley was distraught over what happened. He asked me

if he could speak to the players after a practice, which I let him do. He brought with him mechanics, pilots, and film to prove the safety of the plane. He added that they had never had any kind of experience like that before. About two weeks later we had a preseason game in San Antonio, and Charley again offered the services of his plane so that we could fly back and forth the same day. To a man, the players refused. We flew commercial instead.

Seeing celebrities, whether they were future presidents, in witness protection programs, or country singers, was nice, but the main thing I had in mind was coaching the professional basketball players who were the 1989–90 Dallas Mavericks. The team I inherited as an interim was already without Roy Tarpley, who was suspended indefinitely on November 16, 1989, for driving while intoxicated. It was the beginning of a slow, steady downward spiral for Roy. He was already battling drug problems—cocaine, primarily—before the season started and had gone to former NBA player John Lucas's rehab center in Houston. I spent time with Roy there, trying to help him beat his addictions, sitting with him in his drug counseling meetings. Roy and I had gotten close, and his wife, Dawn, and my future wife, Carol, also became friends. Because of all my years working with inner-city kids in New Jersey, I felt I had an ability to relate and connect with Roy, and I knew he could see in me a guy who cared about him as a person, not just somebody who could help me win basketball games.

On the night Roy was arrested, he was on the Belt Line, the main highway that loops around Dallas, and he was pulled over by one of those hardcore Dallas cops. Back then, a fashionable thing to have was these leather pocketbooks Nike was giving everyone. I had one, too. When the cop asked Roy for his license and registration, Roy told him it was in the trunk—in that Nike pocketbook. The cop told him not to go into the trunk, telling him instead to stay put. Roy didn't listen. He got out of the car, this seven-foot guy, and started going to the trunk. That's when the cop grabbed him, and from what I understand, he threw Roy against the car, causing him to bang his head. He called for backup, and they arrested him.

I hated to see these incidents and episodes happen to Roy. I hated it first for him, because he really was a good guy, and I hated it for the team, because he was a really good player who needed the structure that being a productive part of a team afforded him. When we had Roy in the lineup, we were very good; when we didn't—not so good. You don't lose a force in the middle of the floor like that and win a lot of games. Tarpley returned briefly that season before he was suspended again for drug use. It crippled us.

I've always believed Roy came into the league ill-equipped to handle the money, the sycophants, the enablers, and especially the temptations. Such a shame, because I believe Roy Tarpley was one of the best ever. There wasn't anything Roy could not do on a basketball court—score, rebound, pass, and defend. I coached Bob Lanier in Detroit. I coached James Donaldson in Dallas. I coached Patrick Ewing and Bill Cartwright in New York. I coached Shaquille O'Neal in Orlando. I coached a lot of big men. Roy was as good as any of them. And he had such personality—smart and witty with a great sense of humor. I could see in Roy the same things I saw in those inner-city kids I worked with—good kids with some bad issues. I felt drawn to Roy, more so than any of my other players. I desperately wanted to help him. Through all of his suspensions I kept in regular contact with him, always trying to help.

Unfortunately, it wasn't just Tarpley we were missing that season. We were riddled with injuries. Our regular lineup of Sam Perkins, Adrian Dantley, Rolando Blackman, Derek Harper, and James Donaldson started just two games together.

Sam Perkins was another one of my favorite players—just a sweetheart of a man. He had a freakish wingspan. He was six feet nine, but when he spread his arms it was as if he were a seven-footer. The joke was that Perkins could tie his shoelaces without bending over. He was both a good defender and hard to guard, and an excellent passer when he was double-teamed. I finally figured out a lineup that worked for us down the stretch, and we went 15-7. After MacLeod's 5-6 start, I was able to guide the team to a 42-29 record the rest of the way, getting us into the playoffs.

It was a grind that season, which NBA seasons can often be. You can't get too high or too low. But there was one low, followed by a high that I will never forget. The low came on March 18, 1990, when we suffered a brutal loss to the Detroit Pistons, who at the time were the defending world champions. The Pistons crushed us 114–84 at their place—the Palace at Auburn Hills. Just a year earlier, on February 15, 1989, we had traded Mark Aguirre to Detroit, and for whatever reason he walked onto our team bus as we were getting ready to leave the arena after the game.

"We're coming to your place next week and we're gonna take another win in Dallas," Aguirre said. I'm guessing he was joking, needling his old teammates and buddies. Nevertheless, I knew better and I didn't say a word. Instead, I thought to myself: Aguirre just got me a W next week. He just gave me all the motivation I would need.

Exactly one week later, we met Aguirre and the Pistons at our place, and our guys were fired up. In fact, we won three straight after that little episode on our bus, so we were getting on a bit of a roll. It was a back-and-forth game against the Pistons, down to the wire, with our guys playing ferocious defense. The game was tied at 82–82 in regulation, and we went into overtime. With less than twenty seconds left in OT, Derek Harper nailed a three-pointer to tie the score at 96–96. The Pistons were inbounding the ball, and I put all six feet ten of Herb Williams on the ball and Harper on Isiah Thomas, since I knew the Pistons would try to get the ball either to Isiah or Joe Dumars.

One thing we did on critical inbounds passes like that was make the countdown loud, knowing that the player trying to inbound the ball would tend to panic if he was running out of time. On that play, we shouted: *Five! Four! Two! One!* We left out the *Three!* on purpose, knowing it could cause the inbound passer to lose concentration and panic. Sure enough, the inbound pass was a frantic attempt to beat the clock, with Herbie reading it perfectly. He slapped the ball away and Harper scooped it up, raced down court, and made the winning basket with just seconds to spare. We had beaten the defending world champion "Bad Boy" Pistons, 98–96.

The momentum carried us, and we won two more games after that. When we finished with five wins in our last six games to make the playoffs, it was all that ownership needed to see. Right after we clinched that playoff berth, the Mavericks announced that I would be the head coach on a permanent basis. It was one of the happiest days of my life. I felt respected, that ownership and management appreciated my hard work and how I dealt with the problems we faced—particularly with Roy Tarpley being in and out of the roster all season.

Our first-round opponent was a tough Portland Trail Blazers team that feature Clyde Drexler, Terry Porter, Jerome Kersey, Buck Williams, and Kevin Duckworth. They swept us in all four games we played in the regular season. As you would imagine, they swept us all three games in the playoffs. That's basketball. That's sports.

There was a well-respected magazine at the time called *Basketball America*, which had a rating system called "The Coaching Index," which ranked the NBA's head coaches. That off-season, they rated me the NBA's second-best coach behind Chuck Daly. I felt that it was further confirmation that I had not only arrived but also established myself in the league.

But no matter how good a coach is, he still needs players. So it was foreboding to me that off-season when Sam Perkins became a free agent and ownership decided not to keep him. They said they were concerned about his knees. I wasn't concerned about his knees, and neither were the Los Angeles Lakers, who signed him to a six-year, $18 million contract. Perkins played all of those six years and another five in the NBA. His knees held up fine. I knew losing Perkins was going to hurt, and Roy Tarpley's situation was always tenuous. We never knew when he would fall off the wagon and go on a binge of cocaine or alcohol—or both. By now, though, I was feeling comfortable and more secure with being in the NBA. I felt I had finally established myself in the league and wouldn't have to ever worry about going back to teaching and coaching inner-city kids in Jersey. I loved those kids and poured my heart into helping them, but I obviously loved the NBA life much, much more.

My personal life was looking up, too. I had met a woman named Carol Begerow, who did a lot of work in local theater, and we really hit it off. She was funny and outgoing, a real people person with an outsized personality—sort of like me. We moved in together and eventually decided to make our relationship official.

At the time, I was doing a lot of off-season clinics for the NBA Coaches Association and somehow latched on to doing them in Italy. When I was still an assistant coach, I took Carol with me on one of those trips, and being the romantic guy that I am, I figured we would get married there. We went to the U.S. Embassy in Rome and tried to fill out all the necessary paperwork. It became a nightmare. So much red tape that we just could not make it happen. But it was a wonderful time. We went from Rome to Milan to Lake Como, which is one of the most beautiful places in the world, situated near the border of Switzerland. Since all our friends knew we were getting married in Italy, I didn't want to return to Texas and have to explain everything, so I started asking around and researching to see if there was a city in Texas named Rome. Heck, I would have settled for any Italian-named city. To my pleasant surprise I discovered that there was a city in Texas named Italy. No joke. Even better is that it was only about an hour south of Dallas. I called the justice of the peace to ask about getting married there and got a hold of a man named Robert H. Roberts.

"No problem," Robert H. Roberts said. "I'm the justice of the peace and the sheriff here. But I have to tell you, it's going to cost you forty-five dollars."

"Forty-five dollars!?" I jokingly exclaimed, as if I were shocked. "Well, I'm going to have to use a credit card."

Carol loved situations like that—just a great sport. As we drove into town I saw the big water tower that said, "Good Luck Italy Gladiators." Gladiators was the nickname for Italy High School. And like everything else in Texas sports, everything revolved around football. I can't say that Italy, Texas, was a one-horse town, since it was more like two horses, which you could still tie to a wooden rail in the downtown area. We found Robert H. Roberts, the town's justice of the peace/sheriff. He was an affable guy with white hair and a matching handlebar mustache. We told him we wanted to get married the next day, at about 6 p.m. It was summertime, steaming hot, and I noticed he didn't have the air conditioner on.

"Can we do something about the air conditioning?" I asked. "Carol is going to be dressed up in a gown, a really beautiful outfit."

"No problem," Robert H. Roberts said. "I'll turn on the air conditioning an hour before the ceremony."

"How long is the ceremony?" I asked.

"About twenty minutes."

"Could you stretch it out a little? Maybe throw in a poem?"

"Sure."

We rented limos and someone from our little entourage brought a boom box to play "Here Comes the Bride."

When Carol came down the aisle to meet me, she was laughing. A good laugh. A happy laugh. Robert H. Roberts saw her and said, "You know, people get very emotional during weddings. They either laugh or cry. I'm glad to see that Carol is laughing."

After "Here Comes the Bride" played on the boom box, the ceremony got under way. When it came time to read a poem, Robert H. Roberts said:

Roses are red
Violets are blue
Sugar is sweet
And so are you

It was hard for us not to burst out laughing. Meanwhile, word spread that a Mavericks coach was getting married that day, and a lot of townspeople turned out for it. We gave them confetti to throw. It was great fun. From there, we rode the limos back to Dallas, had a wonderful dinner, and then met a lot of friends and some of my players at a discotheque.

The next day, a newspaper headline read: "Adubato Gets Married in Italy; Italy, Texas That Is . . ."

Mission accomplished. Carol and I still laugh about that to this day, always telling people we got married in Italy . . . Texas.

I was in love with my wife, loved living in Dallas, loved being a bona fide NBA coach, loved my life—and then there was the team. I don't care who you are. I don't care if you are a combination of John Wooden, Mike Krzyzewski, Phil Jackson, and Pat Riley, if you don't have the players, you're not going to win. And we didn't have the players. (Speaking of Pat Riley, as a side note, Riley was born in Rome . . . New York.)

We started that 1990–91 season with promise, winning four of our first five games. Roy Tarpley was a force. Our third game of the season we were playing the New York Knicks at Madison Square Garden, and I pulled Tarpley aside and gave him an impassioned pep talk. "Listen Roy," I said, "this is Madison Square Garden, the Mecca of basketball—college and pros. This is where you make a name for yourself. You're going against Patrick Ewing tonight, one of the all-time great centers. I was with Patrick when he came to New York. He's a great player. But I think you're better. You just need to play hard, stay out of foul trouble, and you'll prove to the world that you're the best in the game."

Tarpley had come into that season overweight, which concerned some people. But it didn't bother me, because to me that meant he was staying away from the drugs. I also knew that the weight would peel off during the grind of an NBA season.

Sure enough, Tarpley played like a crazed man that night, really getting after it and at the same time getting on Ewing's nerves. In the second quarter there was a rebound that both Tarpley and Ewing battled for. Since Ewing had him boxed out,

Tarpley went over him. As he grabbed the basketball he came down on Ewing, knocking him to the floor. Ewing jumped up and squared off to fight. I raced onto the court and got between these two giants. Since I had a relationship with Ewing, I appealed to him that it was going to be all right, but he was fairly worked up.

"Richie, he tried to strangle me!" he said. "He's crazy!"

I kept talking to Patrick, and eventually I somehow managed to calm him down. Meanwhile, Roy was at the other side of the court, and when I got to him I could see he was still worked up.

"Roy, Roy, you gotta relax! This is the place to make it. Show him you're a better player. I know you can kick his ass. You don't need to fight him to prove that. Just go out there and outplay him."

"Coach, you know I can kick his ass?" he asked.

"Absolutely!"

"Okay," he said, and I could see a calm come over him. "I'm all right, then."

What a show Roy and Patrick put on after that. Roy finished with 29 points, 10 rebounds, and 3 blocked shots, while Patrick poured in 26 points, grabbed 10 rebounds, and blocked 6 shots. The best stat of all, though, is that we won, 96–91.

The next night we were playing the 76ers in Philadelphia, and again Tarpley was just a beast. This time, however, it was Charles Barkley who didn't appreciate his aggressiveness. Sure enough, after one battle beneath the boards, the two big men squared off. I didn't know Charles the way I did Patrick, so there wasn't much I could do to soothe Barkley. Plus, there was a part of me that was sort of curious to see how the two of them would box it out. But thankfully, I guess, that never happened. The game resumed and we won, 104–101, with Tarpley leading both teams in scoring, with 26 points, and in rebounds, with 11.

But our season soon unraveled after that. We lost our key guard, Lafayette "Fat" Lever, to a knee injury in that 76ers game, resulting in season-ending surgery. One game later, we lost Tarpley to a torn anterior cruciate ligament, and he was out for the season. We never recovered from losing our two best players. Fat played in all of four games, and Roy in five. An NBA season is eighty-two games. That kind of math is easy to do. Problem was, it led to this math—a 28-54 regular-season record.

Losing gets to you, and a lot of times you take it out on the officials. It's human nature. And the one thing about being a head coach is that it's a whole different relationship with the officials. As an assistant coach you're mostly working behind the scenes, and while you might say a few things from the bench, it's really not your place. But when you're the head coach, you're out front, arguing calls, fighting for your players. Being a Jersey Guy, I could get on an official with the best of them. But there was one referee, Ed Rush, who always seemed to have it in for me. There were two referees named Ed Rush in the NBA—Ed, who is white, and Eddie Rush, who is black. Ed Rush was from Philadelphia and he seemed to have it in for any of us Jersey Guys. He didn't like Hubie Brown or Dick Vitale, and that seemed to carry over to me.

One night in a game Ed Rush was officiating, I told my two assistants, Bob Zuffelato and Gar Heard, "I'm not even going to look at Ed Rush tonight. I don't wanna gamble that he's gonna give us a bad call. I'm just going to sit here and coach the game and not even worry about him."

No matter what the bad call was, I didn't say a word. But it was hard to keep my bench quiet. On one particular bad call, a foul against us, one of our bench guys correctly thought that there was a travel by the other team before the foul was called against us. So as their guy went to the foul line, our guy from the bench stood up and rolled his arms, signaling traveling. Rush was under the basket, ready to toss the ball to their guy to shoot the foul shots, when he saw my bench guy making the traveling call motion with his arms. Immediately Rush beelined to our bench and called a technical foul on my guy. Still, I said nothing. But that wasn't good enough for Rush. As he headed back down the floor, he stopped, looked at me, and said, "And I'm taking none of your shit tonight, Richie!" I was seething. But I just sat there, passive.

We lost that night, a close game, and it really stung. As we were walking to our locker room, the three officials walked past us. At that point I couldn't help myself. Looking at Rush, I shouted, "Hey Ed, you got me again!" He turned and gave me this big grin, as if to say, *You bet I did.* For a second, I stood there stunned. Then I went after him. Rush took off running. I chased him all the way to the officials' locker room, but before I could get to him, one of the other officials, Bob Delaney, an ex-New Jersey State Police officer from Paterson, tackled me. As Delaney was yelling "Calm down, Richie! Calm down!" Rush slammed the door shut and shouted, "Richie, you know you're gonna get fined like you can't believe!" And I did, to the tune of $3,500.

About a week or so later, I had another issue with another official. This one was Ron Garretson, whose father, Darell, was the head of the officials. Right before halftime, one of our players went up for a desperation shot from half court and he got sandwiched between two opposing players and knocked to the ground. The shot got off before the buzzer, but Garretson didn't call it. As we walked off the court, I turned to him and said, "Ronnie, that shot went off before the buzzer. In fact, the ball hit the floor before the buzzer went off."

He turned to me and said, "Obviously, I don't think so."

And I said, "Obviously, you're blind."

When we came out after halftime, I learned that a technical foul had been assessed to me before the start of the third quarter. Again, I was seething. We lost that game, too, another close one that came down to a non-call against the other team. In coaching vernacular, that's what we call "swallowing the whistle."

After the game I was shouting at Garretson, angrily tailing him all the way to the officials' locker room. Another no-no, and another $3,500 fine. Our team owner used to pay my fines, usually about $250 to $500, but $7,000 in the span of about a week had even our owner mad at me, especially since my antics were also getting me—and the franchise—bad publicity in the media. So he said he wasn't going to pay for these fines. Luckily, Rod Thorn, the NBA's VP of basketball operations and the league disciplinarian, was a friend of mine. "Richie, I took $3,500 from you last week. I can't take another $3,500 from you this week." But he did. After the season, though, I got a check back for $3,500. Thorn had taken care of one of the fines. The other one I still had to pay myself.

The 1991–92 season got off to an ominous start. Recovering from his knee surgery from the previous season, Tarpley had too much time on his hands away from the structure of a team. Sure enough, he got back on the drugs. On October 16, during training camp, before the season even started, Tarpley violated the NBA's substance abuse policy for a third time, and he was banned from the league. I was devastated for Roy, and it devastated our chances that season. Fat Lever was still hampered by his knee issues, and he missed most of the season and was never the same player again. We lost six of our first seven games and could never seem to get it going. One step forward two steps back? Nah. It was more like one step forward five steps back.

It's hard as a head coach to keep players motivated when they know they are not going to make the playoffs and the season is winding down and everyone is tired, battling aches and pains. On February 20, 1992, we traded our seven-foot-two center, James Donaldson, which really hurt, too. We were going nowhere—fast. As we limped to the finish line, we had one really horrific stretch when we lost fifteen straight games. It was awful.

One day, when I went to church, I tried to keep a low profile. I wanted to get in and out without anybody noticing and certainly without anybody asking about our season. So I sat in the last pew, all the way in the back, hoping nobody would see me. When the priest got up to deliver his sermon he said: "Yesterday, I went to the grocery store. After I walked inside I realized I had left my car unlocked with two Mavericks tickets sitting on the front seat. I immediately got nervous and ran back outside. When I got to my car, I opened the door and there, sitting on my seat, were four Mavericks tickets." The church erupted with laughter, and then everyone turned to look at me. I guess, as with our losing streak, I had not gone unnoticed.

We finished 22-60, and yet somehow I survived to coach another year. That wasn't necessarily a good thing, though, because we didn't improve our personnel that off-season. After we started the 1992–93 season with a 2-27 record I couldn't take all the losing anymore. No matter where I coached before, I'd always won. But as any coach can tell you, you're only as good as your talent.

We were heading to Detroit to play the powerhouse Pistons, and I met with our vice president of operations Rick Sund and asked him if he could do me a big favor.

"What's that?" he asked.

"Rick," I said, "this is a CBA team playing in the NBA. Please fire me."

I knew I could say something that blunt to him because we had a great relationship.

"C'mon Richie, you can get through this year," he said.

"I'm telling you, Rick, there's gonna be a lot of suffering this year. So if you want to fire me, that's okay. Don't worry about it."

We talked a little more and Rick tried to reassure me. Once we got to Detroit, I looked forward to seeing a couple of my Jersey Guys—Mike Fratello and Ron Rothstein. Fratello was on the broadcasting team for TNT and Rothstein was the Pistons' head coach. The night before the game, we went out to dinner.

"I can't take it anymore," I told them. As Rick had done the day before, they tried to reassure me. That got me thinking, and I remembered that Rick was supposed to join us for dinner, but he didn't show up. Just then, I saw hanging on the wall of the restaurant a huge copy of *The Last Supper*. "Look, we're under *The Last Supper*! That's a sign! I'm gonna get fired tomorrow! That's why Rick didn't meet us for dinner."

The next morning, Sund called me in my hotel room. "Richie, we have to meet," he said. He came to my room, knocked on my door, and when I opened it I could see that Rick was crying.

"Rick, what's up?" I said, as if I didn't know.

"Richie, I have to fire you."

I gave him a hug. "Rick, don't feel bad. You're doing me a favor."

Gar Heard took over, won the first game, and then lost nineteen games in a row. They went on to finish 9-44 the rest of the way. Quinn Buckner took over as head coach before the following season, in 1993–94, and Dallas went 13-69. In fact, it wouldn't be until the 2000–2001 season, which was the first season with Mark Cuban as the franchise's new owner, that the Mavericks turned in a winning record. By then, I was the head coach in the fledgling WNBA. But I wasn't done with the NBA, nor the NBA with me. Not by a long shot.

1. My senior picture from
Clifford J. Scott High School
in East Orange, New Jersey.
Courtesy of the Adubato family.

2. Baseball was my other passion. I played first base on my Paterson College team. Courtesy of the Adubato family.

3. I was a left-handed shooter who played point guard for Paterson College, which is now called William Paterson University. I was good enough to make the school's Hall of Fame in basketball and baseball. Courtesy of the Adubato family.

4. I coached a lot of basketball camps with a lot of big names in coaching. This is a group photo at the Hubie Brown Summer Camp. I'm second from the left in the front row, between Brendan Suhr and Mike Fratello. Hubie Brown is third from the right in the back row. Courtesy of the Adubato family.

5. What a great player Derek Harper was, especially on defense, which I loved coaching. Courtesy of the Adubato family.

6. With Patrick Ewing before a game in
Orlando, when I was an assistant coach
with the Orlando Magic and Patrick was
en route to a Hall of Fame career with
the New York Knicks. Courtesy of the
Adubato family.

7. I didn't think I would get another NBA head-coaching job after the Detroit Pistons, but in 1989 I became the Dallas Mavericks' head coach. Focus On Sport/Getty Images Sport/Getty Images.

8. I could get vocal with the officials when I was the Dallas Mavericks' head coach, which could lead to some hefty fines. Seated to my right is our trainer, Doug Atkinson. Courtesy of the Adubato family.

9. My buddy Dick Vitale is also a big baseball junkie. When I was the Dallas Mavericks' head coach, Bobby Valentine was the Texas Rangers' manager. We had a little fraternity going. Courtesy of the Adubato family.

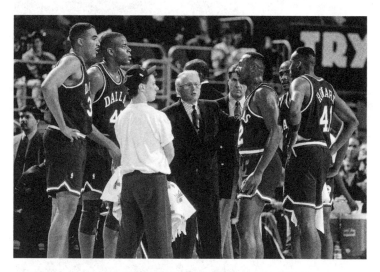

10. Here I am in a team huddle, coaching the Dallas Mavericks at my old stomping grounds—Madison Square Garden. Nathaniel S. Butler/ National Basketball Association/Getty Images.

11. Another photo of me coaching the Dallas Mavericks at Madison Square Garden. Seated to my left are our trainer, Doug Atkinson, and my assistant coaches, Bob Zuffelato and Gar Heard. Nathaniel S. Butler/ National Basketball Association/Getty Images.

12. I am frantically calling a timeout while coaching the Dallas Mavericks. Behind me is one of my assistant coaches, Bob Zuffelato. Nathaniel S. Butler/National Basketball Association/Getty Images.

13. (*opposite top*) Two great guys and NBA players: Sam Perkins to my right and Detlef Schrempf to my left, posing with my son Adam. Courtesy of the Adubato family.

14. (*opposite bottom*) At the White House in 1988 with Roy Tarpley (to my right) and Detlef Schrempf (to my left). Tarpley's tragic death still haunts me. Courtesy of the Adubato family.

15. (*above*) Carol and I the day we got married in Italy . . . Texas: July 25, 1989. Courtesy of the Adubato family.

16. The Orlando Magic advanced to the NBA Finals in 1995, when I was an assistant coach under my former high school player Brian Hill. Fernando Medina/National Basketball Association/ Getty Images.

17. My last NBA head-coaching stop was with the Orlando Magic, the franchise I have been most identified with and still work for as a broadcaster. Courtesy of the *Orlando Sentinel*.

18. During the 1994–95 season, when the Orlando Magic won the Eastern Conference Finals, I was an assistant coach and regularly in the ear of Shaquille O'Neal. Courtesy of the Adubato family.

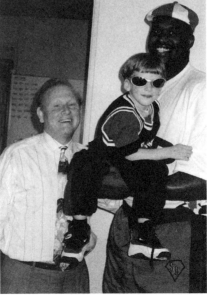

19. Shaquille O'Neal has always been great with kids. Here he is holding up my son Adam, who is also wearing Shaquille's glasses. Adam was four years old. Courtesy of the Adubato family.

20. (*opposite top*) Shaquille O'Neal was one of my all-time favorite players, full of personality. Here we are in my office with Dick Vitale and Vitale's wife, Lorraine, and daughter, Sherri. Courtesy of the Adubato family.

21. (*opposite bottom*) My son Adam, Dick Vitale, and I, posing with the great Penny Hardaway, who has gone on to become a college head coach. Courtesy of the Adubato family.

22. (*above*) Dick Vitale is one of my oldest and closest friends. We have enjoyed many meals and laughs together. Here we are at a restaurant in 1996. Courtesy of the Adubato family.

23. At a gala celebrating the grand reopening of Radio City Music Hall. Here I am with the actress Ann-Margaret, who is obviously making a point with me. Courtesy of the Adubato family.

24. In 1999, when Ernie Grunfeld hired me to coach the WNBA's New York Liberty. I loved coaching the women's game. Courtesy of the Adubato family.

25. In 1999 I embarked on a new journey, which was coaching the New York Liberty in the WNBA. We went all the way to the WNBA Finals, where we lost to the juggernaut that was the Houston Comets. Fernando Medina/ National Basketball Association/Getty Images.

26. One of the smartest and best players I coached with the New York Liberty was Becky Hammon, who is now making history as an NBA assistant coach. Mitchell Layton/National Basketball Association/ Getty Images.

1999, 2000, 2002 EASTERN CONFERENCE CHAMPIONS

27. I had six wonderful seasons coaching the New York Liberty—from 1999 to 2004. I am proud of the three Eastern Conference Championships we won during that time. Courtesy of the Adubato family.

28. I was always ultra-prepared before games, but I also prided myself on being an in-game tactician. Here I am in a courtside huddle with my Washington Mystics players. Behind me, to my right, are my two assistant coaches, the appropriately named Tree Rollins and Marynell Meadors. Mitchell Layton/National Basketball Association/Getty Images.

29. Here I am as the Washington Mystics' head coach, calling a triangle-three play against the Houston Comets, which would hopefully result in a successful three-point bucket. Mitchell Layton/ National Basketball Association/Getty Images.

30. I was the head coach of three WNBA All-Star teams. Here I am on the sidelines in Phoenix in 2000, coaching the Eastern Conference All-Stars. Barry Gossage/ National Basketball Association/Getty Images.

31. Standing at Moscow's Red Square
with my agent, Bruce Levy. Some of the
highlights of my international coaching
career came in Russia. Courtesy of the
Adubato family.

32. With the two female loves of my life—my wife, Carol, and my daughter, Beth. Courtesy of the Adubato family.

33. Flanked by my two sons, Scott (to my right) and Adam (to my left), and, of course, my wife, Carol. We were at one of Dick Vitale's fundraising events for pediatric cancer. Courtesy of the Adubato family.

34. I have partnered in broadcasting Orlando Magic games with my friend Dennis Neumann, an ultimate pro and one of the best play-by-play guys I have ever heard. Courtesy of the *Orlando Sentinel*.

35. The year 2020 marked my sixtieth consecutive year in basketball, where, in addition to broadcasting, I have coached high school, college, NBA, WNBA, and internationally. Through all those decades and all the games, I have never stopped havin' a ball. Courtesy of the Adubato family.

9

Orlando by Way of Cleveland

I knew I wasn't done with the NBA. More importantly, I knew the NBA wasn't done with me. I didn't know where my next job in the league would come from, but I was confident it would come from somewhere. Sure enough, the Jersey Guys pulled me back in again. This time it was Mike Fratello who called. Fratello, who grew up in Hackensack, New Jersey, had come a long way from that night when, as high school coaches, we were arguing in the street with trash cans about how best to defend the pick and roll. After Fratello and I coached together as assistants for Hubie Brown and the New York Knicks, he became the Atlanta Hawks' head coach from 1983 to 1990. In 1993 he got the Cleveland Cavaliers head-coaching job, and he hired our buddy Ron Rothstein and me to be his assistants.

My first day on the job was the day of the NBA Draft. That was also the first day I met the Cavs' owner, Gordon Gund, who is legally blind. Before Gund came into what we call the war room, Fratello pulled me and Rothstein aside, just to make sure we knew about Gund's condition. "Please don't say anything related to anybody being blind, or make any comments like that," he said. I looked at Fratello incredulous. "Of course not," I said. "We would never do anything like that."

The NBA Draft is a long and frenetic day. You get inside that war room the first thing in the morning and it's nonstop with phones ringing and split-second decisions to be made. Every decision every team makes has a domino effect. And nothing goes as planned. It's like being in a bunker where you never see the light of the sun.

Late in the day they brought us a catered dinner and left it in the hallway. Since nobody was bringing it in, Rothstein and I went to get the food, only to discover that it was encased in plastic. We thought it might be easy to get it off, but it wasn't. Ron would try something, I would try something, but nothing seemed to get that plastic off. It wasn't until we employed knives and scissors that we were able to methodically free the food from that plastic wrapping. It took a while, but we were hungry and therefore persistent.

When we brought the food into the war room, Fratello looked at us quizzically and asked, "Where were you guys? You've been gone for like forty-five minutes."

"You wouldn't believe how tough it was to get the plastic off all this food," I said. "Ronnie and I were trying everything. It was like the blind leading the blind."

The room went silent. I don't think I've ever heard a silence as loud as that silence was. I . . . was . . . horrified.

Turning around to where he knew I was standing, Gund smiled and said, "Can I join that club?" Everybody busted out laughing, and I breathed a sigh of relief.

Later on, when we were talking about a player we all liked, Rothstein said excitedly, "You should *see* how he shoots from the three-point range." Everybody got quiet again. Gund immediately laughed and all was good. What a first day. And what a great guy our owner was.

Unfortunately, our season was no laughing matter. The Cavs, like everyone else in the NBA, could not get past Michael Jordan and the Chicago Bulls. Unlike a lot of other teams in the league, we felt we had the talent to break through—players like Brad Daugherty, John "Hot Rod" Williams, Mark Price, Larry Nance, and Gerald Wilkins. After always seeming to be in a rebuilding situation, Rothstein and I were excited about being in a situation where we were helping a playoff caliber team get better. More than anything, we loved to teach. And we had some good students.

But things did not start well. We lost fourteen of our first twenty-one games as injuries to two of our big guys took their toll. Daugherty, our center, had back problems, and Nance, our power forward, was hampered by a knee injury. We still managed a winning record, going 47-35, but we were swept in the first round by—who else?—Michael Jordan and the Chicago Bulls.

I enjoyed working with Fratello, who isn't just one of my best friends in basketball, but one of my best friends—period. Like me, he started his career as the freshmen coach at Hackensack High School. He is also the godfather to Adam Adubato—my son with Carol. You can imagine then, how torn I was when another one of my Jersey boys, Brian Hill, called me after the season and asked if I would be his assistant coach with the Orlando Magic. As well as I knew Fratello, the same was true with Brian Hill, who had played for me in high school, at Our Lady of the Valley.

I was intrigued by what the Magic were doing in Orlando. Really, who wouldn't be? They had a young, dynamic team with Shaquille O'Neal at center, Dennis Scott at forward, and Nick Anderson and Penny Hardaway at the guard positions. This was clearly a dynasty in the making. I told Fratello about Brian's interest and that I wanted to go talk to him. "Go ahead," he said, without any malice. I knew Fratello only wanted the best for me, and I appreciated that.

I had a great visit with Brian in the off-season of 1994, but I was still torn. On the way back to Cleveland, I happened to be on the same flight as Brad Daugherty. We were sitting at the gate talking, and at one point he said, "Coach, I'm going to get some coffee. You want a cup?" I said yes, and when Brad got up he winced. It was obvious that his back, which had hampered him and kept him on the sidelines for a chunk of the previous season, was getting worse. A little while later, when we were called to board the plane, Brad winced again when he tried to unfold himself from his seat, this time with an audible groan. He could not even stand. I took it as a sign that he was done—and he was. Brad Daugherty never played another NBA game. I was also hearing rumblings that, because of his knee, Larry Nance was done. And he was. He also never played another NBA game.

What once looked like a promising situation in Cleveland was now looking like another rebuilding project. Plus, my wife Carol was tired of the freezing winter weather in Cleveland. I decided to head south to the warm weather in Orlando and to a hot young team in the Magic, which had also just signed Horace Grant as a free agent to play power forward. I thought he was the last piece of a championship puzzle, and perhaps even the beginning of a dynasty.

It was obvious when I got to Orlando that this was Shaquille O'Neal's team. Later, Shaq and Penny each became jealous of the attention the other was getting, which was so unfortunate. But make no mistake, this was Shaq's team. In just his third year in the league, he was a force. Unless you saw Shaq day after day, you could not fully appreciate just how freakishly athletic he was at seven feet one and 325 pounds. He wasn't just big; he was bigger than life, with a big personality.

There was one game that season when we were supposed to play the 76ers in Philadelphia, but because of a bad snowstorm we were forced to land at the Lehigh Valley International Airport and stay at a local Holiday Inn. Stranded at the same hotel were a band of freaks—that is, they were freaks as far as I was concerned. I asked someone who they were and why there was such a commotion about them, and I was told it was a popular musician named Marilyn Manson and his band. I instinctively knew this wasn't going to be good. And guess who knew them personally? Shaq. When he saw Marilyn Manson, who was in full freak makeup, he walked over and picked him up off the ground. With one hand. Then Shaq spun him around over his head. Everyone thought it was hilarious. I'll admit, I laughed too. But there were little warning bells in my head telling me that this hotel stay wasn't going to go very well.

Sure enough, those warning bells went off at about one in the morning. I was asleep in my room when the fire alarm began blaring. Here we go, I thought. I ran into the hallway and saw Brian Hill and two of our other assistant coaches, Tree Rollins and Tom Sterner, standing around and looking as tired and bewildered as I was. After a while, when we could see that nothing dangerous was happening, that it evidently was a false alarm, the guys went back to their rooms on the fourth floor, and I got to thinking about the freaks I had seen earlier in the evening—and I had a bad feeling.

I saw a couple of players in the hallway, and we decided that to be safe we would head to the lobby. Sure enough, on the way down we were joined by Marilyn Manson and his band—still in full freak makeup. Why, of course, I thought. Why wouldn't we run into them in the middle of the night? Don't all horror movies progress like this? And I don't say that lightly. The way they looked felt creepy to me, if not scary. It felt like Halloween night, except it wasn't October 31.

It turned out that the fire alarm was triggered by too much smoke in the kitchen, but I still did not feel comfortable. I turned to one of the players and said, only half jokingly, "I think we're in hell. Just look around. There's the devil and his disciples." I went back to my room, but I didn't sleep well the rest of the night. Thankfully, nothing else happened, and I was glad when we got the hell out of there and back to the business of playing basketball.

That 1994–95 season was a great one, and there were a few times when I had to step back and remind myself that not only was I in the NBA, but now I was on a staff coaching some of the league's best young talent. As good as Shaq was, though, his Achilles' heel was his foul shooting. One of the writers covering the team, Bill Fay of the *Tampa Tribune*, wrote a fairly in-depth article detailing just how bad not only Shaq was from the line, but how bad his form was—how he pushed the ball instead of shooting it, how he didn't get his legs into it, and just how atrocious his free-throw percentage was.

The next night, Shaq drove the lane and then allowed his momentum to carry him into the press section, which was underneath the basket along the baseline. All 325 pounds of sweaty Shaq went right into where the media were sitting, specifically toward one guy—Bill Fay. He brushed against Fay and, of course, Shaq made it seem like an accident, but it wasn't. As he grabbed Fay's shoulder and used it as leverage to get up, Shaq whispered into his ear, "If you write one more article about my foul shooting, the next time you're going to have this Shaq-mobile land right on top of you." With that, he walked away wearing that trademark crooked grin on his face. Classic Shaq.

It was a great season. A lot of fun. When you're winning, it's always fun. And we won the Atlantic Division with a 57-25 record. In the first round of the playoffs we handled the Boston Celtics easily, beating them 3–1. Up next was the team that shattered so many dreams of so many other teams in the '90s—the Chicago Bulls. This was a different Chicago Bulls team, though. This was a Bulls team with a rusty Michael Jordan, still trying to work his way back into basketball form after his year-plus foray into professional baseball. Prior to the start of the playoffs Jordan had only played in the Bulls' final seventeen regular-season games, so it was only natural that he would still be a bit rusty. Not that I was complaining. I wanted to finally beat the Bulls in the playoffs, and this was about as good of an opportunity as we were going to get.

It was a back-and-forth series. The first two games were on our court, and we took Game One in dramatic fashion. As rusty as Jordan was, he was on fire much of that series. But in Game One he was mortal. Not only did Jordan score only 19 points, but one of the most embarrassing moments in his career happened with seconds left in the game and the Bulls up by a point. Jordan was dribbling the ball up court when Nick Anderson, who grew up in Chicago, raced up behind him and tipped the ball to Penny Hardaway—leaving Jordan sprawled helpless on the court. Penny immediately went on a fast break before bounce passing the ball to Horace Grant, and with 6.2 seconds left, Horace stuffed the ball home with what proved to be the winning points. It was a big victory, but it was also a big wakeup call for Jordan, who roared back with 38, 40, 26, 39, and 24 points in Games Two through Six. But we still prevailed, winning the series 4–2.

It was beyond gratifying. Finally, I was on the coaching staff of a team with dynamic talent; a team that had just beaten Michael Jordan and the Chicago Bulls.

But there wasn't much time to celebrate. Next on the agenda were the Indiana Pacers for the Eastern Conference Finals and the right to advance to the NBA Finals. It was a ferocious seven-game series, and every step of the way I could not help but think about how the Pacers' superstar player was that skinny UCLA kid named Reggie Miller, who years earlier told me to keep an eye on him because he was going to become a great NBA player. Boy, was he right. Again and again, Reggie sank clutch baskets when the Pacers needed them the most. And while we had Shaq, they had a great center in Rik Smits. Plus they were a physical team. Also, not to be overlooked was the fact that their coach was Larry Brown, one of the all-time best technicians and teachers of the game. It was a grind, but we beat the Pacers in a deciding seventh-game blowout. It was exhilarating. Here we were, this young franchise that had never in its brief history even so much as won a playoff game, and now we were going to the NBA Finals.

Our reward for that feat was the defending NBA champion Houston Rockets. Their center was Hakeem "The Dream" Olajuwon, who was the best in the NBA. I think Shaq would admit that, as young as he was at the time, he was a little bit in awe of a great veteran like Olajuwon. It wasn't just that Olajuwon was incredibly talented, he also was strong and aggressive, and he had the kind of desire you can't coach into a player. He also had incredible footwork for a center. Olajuwon had played soccer before setting his sights on basketball, and it showed. He had every move in the book—jump hooks, up and unders, baseline drives, reverse layups, and, of course, a monster dunk. Then there was Clyde "The Glide" Drexler. For my money, Drexler was a step behind Jordan. And I do mean only a step. What a wonderful all-around player he was. Had Drexler played in a major market like New York, Chicago, or Los Angeles, he would have gotten a lot more notoriety and accolades, which he richly deserved.

As good as Houston was, we had a better record during the regular season. In fact, the Rockets finished only third in the Midwest Division, with a 47-35 record, while our 57-25 record won us the Atlantic Division. In retrospect, we had a young team that was overconfident. Years later, an *Orlando Sentinel* story talked about how Shaq and the guys were overconfident and partied hard before the NBA Finals, which is something Shaq called a "lost opportunity."

As it turns out, Game One was pivotal—not only for the Finals but for Magic franchise history. We had that game won when, in the closing seconds, leading by 3 points, Nick Anderson missed four consecutive free throws. I felt devastated for him. We all did. Sometimes, even with world-class athletes, the moment overwhelms them. When Houston's Kenny Smith hit a clutch three-pointer to send the game into overtime, we all had a foreboding feeling. My mind flashed back thirty years earlier, to 1965, when I was a high school head coach at Our Lady of the Valley and we won the North Jersey State Championship. We were in Atlantic City, playing St. Rose Belmar, the South Jersey State Champions, for the Parochial B State Championship. In the last ten seconds of the game I had two different players miss a pair of free throws—that's *four* free throws total—to send the game into overtime, and we ended up losing on a free throw.

This was different, of course. This was the NBA Finals. But athletes are athletes, no matter what level you're playing. When something as catastrophic as that happens, it has a ripple effect. It gets inside your head, into your psyche. Poor Nick was not the same player after that, reluctant to drive the lane. Meanwhile, you also could feel the Rockets' experience as the defending champions take over. They won that game, and it set the tone for the series. We lost the first three games and were mentally destroyed going into Game Four, which was at Houston. The Rockets completed the sweep by also beating us in that game, 113–101.

After Game Four, the city had a so-called police escort for our bus back to the airport. I say so-called because, unbelievably, it was just two motorcycle cops. It seemed like the whole city of Houston was in the streets, many seemingly drunk, waving brooms. At a red light—and why we would have to stop at a red light with a police escort is another question—a swarm of fans rushed the bus and started rocking it. Somehow the cops got it under control and we were on our way. In the chaos, though, the bus driver, or the cops, or both, got sidetracked, and we ventured deeper and deeper into the heart of the inner city. Fortunately, Tree Rollins had played for the Rockets and knew the area. So there was Tree, Orlando's assistant coach, telling the bus driver the best way to get the hell out of there, navigating through what felt like a drunken riot in the making. The whole thing had us on edge.

It was a bittersweet feeling going into the off-season. We had just been swept by the defending world champions, which, and there is no way to sugarcoat it, was a big, big disappointment. But we also had a great young team, with a great young center in Shaquille O'Neal, who we were convinced was going to lead us to multiple NBA titles.

Or so we thought.

10

Shaq, We Hardly Knew You

T here is nothing like a basketball gym. To me, it's like church. The head coach is the pastor, the assistant coaches the deacons, the players the parishioners, the rhythmic sound of bouncing basketballs the hymns, and the first day of practice is like a religious holiday. I could not wait for that holiday to arrive in the fall of 1995.

We had our starting five back—Shaquille O'Neal, Penny Hardaway, Horace Grant, Dennis "3-D" Scott, and Nick Anderson. They were still so young, yet now they were armed with the experience of going to the NBA Finals. Shaq was just twenty-three, Penny twenty-four, Horace thirty, 3-D twenty-seven, and Nick twenty-eight. That's a starting five with an average age of twenty-six. We were all eager for the season to begin and to get back to the NBA Finals—and win it.

Sure enough, we roared out of the gate to a 25-6 record and never looked back. It was a historic season, the best regular season the Magic have ever had, and the second-best record in the NBA that season. We won sixty games, lost only twenty-two, and promptly steamrolled the Detroit Pistons in the first round of the playoffs, sweeping them in three games. Then we handled the Atlanta Hawks, beating them four games to one to advance to the Eastern Conference Finals. That's when we encountered the team that actually had the NBA's best record that season, with an even more historic record than our 60-22 mark—the Chicago Bulls, who had gone 72-10 behind a maniacally inspired Michael Jordan.

Evidently, losing to us in the conference semifinals the season before did not sit well with Jordan. Not only did he lead the Bulls to an almost perfect regular-season record, they—like us—had gotten to the Eastern Conference Finals by sweeping their first-round opponent, the Miami Heat, in three games, before beating the New York Knicks four games to one.

Jordan was waiting for us. He *wanted* us. That was clear. After what we had done to him the season before, especially with Nick Anderson embarrassing him with the steal and his former teammate Horace Grant punctuating the ensuing fast break with a one-armed stuff—well, he wanted nothing more than to avenge that. I think Jordan wanted us almost more than he wanted to win the NBA Finals. *Almost.* But that was Michael Jordan; I've never seen a fiercer competitor.

The Bulls blew us out in Game One, 121–83, even though Penny poured in 38 points to lead all scorers. In Game Two, Shaq was the leading scorer with 36 points, while Jordan had 35. It was a closer game, but we still lost, 93–88. Because Jordan was such an offensive force, people tended to overlook just how world-class he was defensively. It showed in Game Three. Jordan led a suffocating Bulls attack against us. We could never get any momentum going offensively, which showed in the fact that Penny was our leading scorer with only 18 points. We lost that game, 86–67.

On the surface, Game Four should have been a foregone conclusion, but I was so proud of our guys. We outscored the Bulls 31–23 in the first quarter and led 56–47 at halftime. But as you would expect, Jordan took over. He finished with 45 points. And when I say he took over, the next leading scorers on the Bulls were Scottie Pippen and Ron Harper, who both had 12 points. Meanwhile Shaq and Penny both led us with 28 points each. It wasn't enough. We lost, 106–101, completing a sweep for the Bulls, who went on to beat the Seattle SuperSonics four games to two, for the first of three more NBA Championships that Chicago would win with Michael Jordan.

That's right, the first of three more NBA Championships. That promising young team that we had, which was led by Shaquille O'Neal, was about to unravel in a historically catastrophic way.

There were already fissures developing between Shaq and Penny. Stupid stuff, but so typical in sports. Whose team was it? Who got the most publicity? Who got the most endorsements? Who got the most credit? Who drove the fancier cars? From a coach's standpoint—who cares?

I love them both, but Shaq, to me, was the greatest. In addition to being a rare talent, he was so fun loving. He would joke around, fool around, but once that ball went up in the air he was all business. Shaq was a tiger on the court. An animal on the glass. He played hard. He played physical. He did it all.

And he wanted to be recognized for it.

Alonzo Mourning had just left the Charlotte Hornets for the Miami Heat, signing a seven-year, $105 million contract. Now it was Shaq's turn, because now he was a free agent. Shaq made it known that he wanted the same contract as Mourning—plus one dollar. He wanted to be recognized as the best center in the NBA, which was the general consensus. Not to take away anything from Mourning, who was a great center, but we're talking about Shaquille O'Neal here.

Though Shaq and Penny were both great players, they were vastly different in one way—Shaq was engaging with his teammates, while Penny tended to be quiet and a bit distant. An NBA season is long, and you need a guy like Shaq who can take control of a locker room as a leader and also keep things loose, cutting through the stress and tension. He was the ultimate motivator. Before games he would have the entire team jumping up and down like pogo sticks, literally bouncing off the walls. If you were anywhere near them it was frightening, like being a mouse trying to avoid stampeding elephants. For the guys, though, it shook loose any pregame jitters and bonded them for battle. That was Shaq, and you never knew what he was going to do next. He had enough nicknames for a whole team, and he loved them all—Superman, Big Diesel, Big Aristotle, The Big Shamrock, and Shaq Foo. He was one of a kind.

Once, when we boarded our team plane, Shaq grabbed the microphone and addressed the team as if they were his troops. Being an army brat growing up, Shaq had spent some time in Germany and knew a little of the language. Slipping into a German accent, he said: "Achtung! Achtung! Everybody vill shut up and listen! Ven you practice I expect 110 percent! Vee vill outhustle every team vee play! And make sure you throw me zee ball in zee low post!" It was hysterical.

Our team plane was a private jet for the Magic, and it had a unique layout. The players sat in the front, the coaches in the middle, and the media in the back. And then way in the back was what we called "Shaq's apartment," with a curtain separating it from the rest of the plane. In that apartment were two seven-foot beds—one for Shaq and the other for his best buddy, Dennis Scott. One night, we were flying from Milwaukee to Chicago and I had a really bad cold. When we boarded the plane, Shaq picked me up, like you would pick up a child, and carried me to the back of the plane, to where his apartment was, and gently laid me in his bed. He pulled the covers up to my neck and tucked me in.

Leaning over my head he said, "You sleep here and get better, because we're gonna need your brains tomorrow night."

Dennis Scott, who was standing next to him, said, "That was a nice thing to do, Shaq."

"Oh Dennis, I forgot to tell you," Shaq said. "You're gonna be sleeping in Richie's seat. I'm taking the other bed—your bed."

As sick as I was, I couldn't help but chuckle.

But that was Shaq. He was a leader, and he took control of situations. Off the basketball court he was still a leader, but at the same time he was funny and engaging, with a heart as big as he was.

I never thought we would lose him. I thought he would be

with the Magic forever. I knew we were in trouble, though, when Magic owner Rich DeVos, who was still relatively new in the big-time world of sports team ownership—he had bought the Magic in 1991—lowballed Shaq with his first contract offer. Not that anybody should sneeze at a $54 million offer spread over four years—the figure which was reported by the *Orlando Sentinel* and other news outlets. It was actually only $1 million less annually than what Alonzo Mourning was getting—*only* $1 million a year being relative, of course. But it still did not have the length or added security that Mourning's contract had, which was a huge mistake. It created an opening for other teams—an opening that was exacerbated by an infamous *Orlando Sentinel* poll.

I was at the Magic offices that day. I wasn't involved in the negotiations, obviously, but I knew Shaq and his team were in a room trying to iron out a contract. At some point, I saw Shaq and his entourage walking down the hallway, looking upset. Shaq's buddy, Dennis Scott, was with him. I briefly stopped Dennis. "3-D, what's wrong?" I asked. Dennis slowed down long enough to tell me, "Oh man, they just screwed up. Shaq is really pissed at the offer."

That summer, the summer of 1996, Shaq had made the U.S. Olympic team. Around that same time, Rich DeVos and the Magic finally saw the light and upped the ante for Shaq. It was reported that they offered $115 million over seven years, which was, at the time, the richest contract ever offered to an NBA player. It was even more than what Michael Jordan was making. That's when the *Orlando Sentinel* did its poll—on the front page of the newspaper!—asking readers: "Is Shaquille O'Neal worth $115 million over 7 seasons?" Keep in mind, not only was Rich DeVos a relatively new owner to big-time sports, the Magic were Orlando's first—and still only—team from one of the four major sports leagues: the NBA, NFL, MLB, and NHL. Safe to say there was a healthy dose of naiveté all the way around as to what it takes to be a major league city.

Some 5,111 people responded to the poll, and a stagger-

SHAQ, WE HARDLY KNEW YOU

ing 91.3 percent of them said no, that Shaq was not worth the money, which also meant that only 8.7 percent said yes. The *Orlando Sentinel* headline blared: "Shaq Attack: Callers Just Say No." In fact, only 49 percent of those polled said that Shaq was even worth his current seven-year, $41 million contract. The responses quoted in the article were typical. A guy named Bill Baker said, "I think the Magic should give the money to the homeless." Yeah right, I thought; as if that is going to happen. The article also quoted a fourteen-year-old girl who trotted out the other obvious clichés (i.e., comparing athletes to doctors who save lives). We all get that, but if we're honest, it's comparing apples to oranges. Another person, someone who sounded like an actual fan, said that only when Shaq played like Michael Jordan should the Magic pay him like Michael Jordan. And on and on it went. Overall, it was bad. Real bad.

Making matters worse was that the Olympic team, Team USA, happened to be training in, of all places, Orlando. Had it been in any other city, his teammates likely would never have known about the poll, since this was back when the internet was still in its infant stages and well before things like social media apps and newspapers were available online. Well, when Shaq's teammates saw the *Orlando Sentinel* poll, they mercilessly teased him—especially Charles Barkley and Scottie Pippen. At the same time, Barkley ripped Magic fans, "They're going to be sorry . . . because they're going to be idiots. They're going to miss him."

There was also a power struggle between Shaq and Brian Hill, which had spilled into the open, especially because Shaq told the media that the team did not respect Brian. There was a second question in the poll that asked whether the Magic should fire Hill if that were one of O'Neal's conditions for returning. Overwhelmingly, 82 percent of the respondents said no.

Adding to all of that was the fact that Shaq was having a child with his girlfriend and—hard to believe nowadays that this would be the case—he was getting hammered in the media and the community for a lack of morals. And finally, there was

Shaq's agent, Leonard Armato, who we all knew wanted his client in the Los Angeles market. Armato got his wish. And so did a lot of misguided people in the Central Florida community. After calling Orlando a "dried-up little pond," Shaq left that pond and headed for a big lake on the Left Coast—the Los Angeles Lakers.

When the news was announced, a local radio station played a remake of the song "Hit the Road Jack," calling it "Hit the Road Shaq."

They were clueless. They had no idea. No idea at all.

11

My Last Go as an NBA Head Coach

S haquille O'Neal never left Orlando. Oh, he did go on to
play for the Los Angeles Lakers, where he would win three
NBA titles; not to mention the NBA title he also won with
the Miami Heat. Shaq still maintains his residence in Orlando.
Even more significantly, he still resides in the damaged psyche of the Orlando Magic and their fans. Make no mistake,
and this is not an overstatement, Shaquille O'Neal leaving
for the Lakers before that 1996–97 season indelibly changed
the course of the Magic, and it is something that to this day
still haunts me.

In real time, though, we could not dwell on Shaq's departure.
We had work to do. Part of that work was finding a replacement at the center position. Not that you are ever going to
replace a Shaquille O'Neal, but we needed something. I went
to our head coach, Brian Hill, and told him I heard that Rony
Seikaly, who was then playing for the Golden State Warriors,
could be available in a trade. I called my good friend Ron Rothstein, who had coached Seikaly with the Miami Heat, and Ron
had a lot of good things to say about him—that he could score,
would get his fair share of rebounds, and also could block a
shot here and there.

But I didn't stop with one recommendation. I called my old
buddy Bob Lanier, whom I had developed a good relationship

with when I was an assistant coach with Detroit and he was the Pistons' center. Lanier in 1994–95 was an assistant coach and an interim head coach with the Warriors, so he saw firsthand what Seikaly had left in the tank. This was a concern because Seikaly was hitting his early thirties, which can be problematic for an NBA player.

"He can still do it on the basketball court," Lanier said. "But there is one problem with Rony."

"What's that?" I asked.

"He's too good-looking," he said. "He dates models. All the other guys on the team are jealous of him."

I laughed my ass off at that one.

We traded for Seikaly and the reports on him proved true. He could still play center—scoring, rebounding, and blocking shots. Oh, and one other thing: he always had gorgeous women around him. In fact, he was always showing the guys pictures of models he was dating and bragging about it. Seikaly later married *Sports Illustrated* swimsuit cover model Elsa Benítez. Not surprisingly, the other guys were jealous of him. Lanier was right.

So, yes, Seikaly was a player in every sense of the word—on and off the court. But as good as he played for us, Rony Seikaly wasn't Shaquille O'Neal. Nobody in the NBA was. Still, we started well enough, going 8-4 in our first twelve games. Then the losing started. And the backbiting. Eventually, we had an ugly and unfortunate coup led by Penny Hardaway and Horace Grant that got my friend Brian Hill, whom I had coached when he was in high school, fired.

After that 8-4 start we went 2-12. Where Shaq had been critical of Brian the season before, it was now Penny who picked up the baton and not only carried it but passed it around to other teammates. It reached a head on February 13, 1997, when we were in Minnesota to play the Timberwolves. Unbeknownst to any of us at the time, Penny called a players-only meeting in his hotel suite. The details of that meeting have since been made public, to the point where Penny was later quoted as telling the *Orlando Sentinel*: "The purpose of the meeting wasn't to discuss how we should fire Coach Hill. But everyone had comments to make and they were all basically negative. We didn't like the offense we were running and we weren't comfortable with the defensive schemes."

To this day I regret that I didn't see any warnings signs, because I would have done something. I would have stepped in before it went too far. Evidently, though, the tipping point came after a February 12 loss to the Pistons in Detroit. There was a heated exchange late in the game between the two Brians—Hill and our other guard, Brian Shaw. I learned later that in the locker room after the game, Hill and Shaw got into a profanity-laced shouting match and that, as this was going on, Penny was pacing, slamming his right fist into his left hand and rolling his head and eyes, clearly agitated. I don't know where I was when this was going on, because I never saw it or heard about it. Maybe I was already on the team bus. And it's not like tempers never flare during the course of a season—either on court or in the locker room—but again, I wish I had known, because I would have stepped in and tried to mitigate whatever tensions there were.

A day after that night in Detroit, when Penny called the players-only meeting in Minneapolis before the Timberwolves game, supposedly, all thirteen players who were present unanimously voted for a change, after which Penny called our general manager, John Gabriel, and told him how they felt.

That night, following the players' meeting, we lost to the Timberwolves, 104–100. Then we lost two more—to the Chicago Bulls, 110–89, and the Charlotte Hornets, 124–110. We were 0-5 since the All-Star break and 24-25 overall, with Penny engaging Gabriel in several more conversations after that first phone call, reiterating the players' displeasure and desire for change. That this was happening after the All-Star break was somewhat significant, because it was later reported that Penny was the object of a lot of needling from some of the guys there—most notably Michael Jordan, Charles Barkley, and Scottie Pippen.

They evidently filled Penny's head with bogus stories that their head coach gave them over-the-top preferential treatment for being superstars—stuff like excusing them from game-day shootarounds. Penny was still young and naive. He bought into all of that—and more. To be fair to Penny, he was also being egged on by Horace Grant, who carried some clout because of the three NBA titles he had helped win with the Chicago Bulls.

When we got back to Orlando from that road trip, the Magic announced Brian Hill's firing. I hate to sound clueless, but I didn't see it coming, and it shook me. In less than a year, we had gone from a young dynasty in the making to a losing record midway through the season and the termination of a dear friend, someone who was not only part of the Jersey Guys but who is like a son to me. What shook me even more was when Gabriel came to me, asking that I take over the team as the head coach. No way, I told him. I could not do that. That's when Brian pulled me to the side. "Look, we know what this business is all about," he told me. "Please don't worry about it. You've gotta take a shot at this. You've gotta take the job."

So I did.

But that's when I came across another shock. When I told management I would take the job, they told me it would only be with an interim tag and that they already had someone in mind to hire in the off-season as their permanent coach. It was, to put it mildly, a tumultuous and confusing transition. I was an NBA head coach again, but there was zero joy in it for me. And it was about to get worse, too.

My first game as the interim head coach was bizarre—a completely different experience from anything I had ever gone through. We were at home against the Portland Trail Blazers, and the fans were worked up. They were aware and angered that there had been a player coup, which the media was now digging into and reporting, and they reacted by lustily booing every one of our starters during the pregame introductions. It was shocking, if not surreal, and I was thankful they did not boo me, too. But they really let the players have it. I cannot imagine that there has ever been a head coach of any team—high school, college, or pro—who has ever had their players booed like that during pregame introductions at home.

In spite of everything, we won that game. Then we won again, and again, and again, and again, and again—stringing together six consecutive wins after coming off a five-game losing streak. Everything started clicking. I was coaching my ass off and the guys really responded by playing hard for me. I'll always believe that one of my intangible strengths as a head coach is an ability to develop a great rapport with players. Penny liked me, believed in me, and you cannot minimize what that means, when a head coach and the star player are simpatico.

Earlier that season, when we were playing the Trail Blazers in Portland, I had gone with Penny and some of the other guys to the Nike factory. Because of his endorsement contract with Nike, Penny was allotted $10,000 worth of merchandise for the day. At one point, I saw that he had three baskets full of stuff and I came up behind him with a couple of baskets that I had.

"Penny," I said, "I'm your favorite coach—right?"

Penny smiled and laughed.

"You want me to take care of you, don't you?" I added.

He laughed again. "Coach, don't worry about it. You're all right. Just get in line with your stuff."

Thanks to Penny, I got Christmas presents for everyone that day. Turns out, Penny was also doing his Christmas shopping. So while I didn't like what Penny had done to Brian Hill, I did like Penny. More importantly, he liked me. Deep down, Penny is a decent, good, and caring man. Since his NBA retirement, he has done a lot of great things in his hometown of Memphis, including coaching high school kids, and now he is the head coach at the University of Memphis.

Penny played hard for me, and for that I will always be grateful. I recall one game, against the New York Knicks at Madison Square Garden, when I felt for sure we didn't have a chance. The Knicks had a powerhouse team, led by Patrick Ewing, and we were shorthanded, playing without Rony Seikaly and Horace

Grant because of injuries. I was prepared to be embarrassed in front of a slew of family and friends whom I had gotten tickets for. But our aging backup center, Danny Schayes, played great, while Penny laid it all on the line—offensively and especially defensively. We won, 93–84, pulling away.

In fact, we won so much that season that after our 24-25 start, we went 21-12, which meant we won 64 percent of our games. To this day, that is the second-best winning percentage out of the thirteen coaches who have ever coached the Magic. Stan Van Gundy, at 66 percent, tops the list.

We were actually 21-9 going into the last three games of the season, when we were scheduled to play the Cavaliers in Cleveland. At the time, the Cavs were coached by my Jersey Guy paisan Mike Fratello. Fratello and the Cavs were battling the Washington Bullets for a playoff spot, so it was a huge game for them. For us, though, it was a meaningless end-of-season game because we had already qualified for the postseason. Since Penny's ankle was barking at him, I sat him. Seikaly had a bum knee, so I sat him too. Part of my logic should have been obvious—I wanted them rested and healthy for the play-offs. Well, the outcry from Washington Bullets fans and from around the country was deafening. The storyline became that I sat two of our best players in order to give my buddy Fratello a better chance to win.

We lost to the Cavs that night, and, as fate would have it, we were scheduled to be in Washington DC two nights later to play the Bullets. Their fans, close to nineteen thousand of them, were all over me, booing and jeering the entire game and holding up signs that said things like: IF FRATELLO HAD FRIENDS LIKE YOU ALL OVER THE NBA HE'D BE 82-0. Penny and Seikaly played that game, but Horace Grant went down early with a wrist injury, and we lost, 104–93.

The last game of the regular season was against a very good Miami Heat team and we were without Horace and Seikaly, whom I decided to rest again. We lost, 102–88, which improved the Heat's record to 61-21, while we finished 45-37. I hardly played Penny that game because early on I could see that they were trying to physically hurt him. Why? Because—again, as fate would have it—we were scheduled to play the Heat in the first round of the playoffs.

We didn't have Horace for any of those games during that playoff series, which made me especially proud of how hard our guys battled. The Heat took the first two games before we bounced back to win the next two, forcing a Game Five, which we lost in Miami.

During that entire series, the media latched onto this narrative that I was out of my league trying to coach against Pat Riley. I'll admit that it bothered the hell out of me. Here we were shorthanded, playing against a team that won sixty-one regular-season games, and we took them to the brink with a Game Five showdown. Not only didn't we have Grant the entire series, but Seikaly, because of a bad knee, hardly played in Game Three and didn't play at all in Games Four or Five. What the media did not bother to research was that I had a good record against Riley as a head coach—when he was coaching the Los Angeles Lakers and I was coaching the Dallas Mavericks. They also did not seem to notice that after losing those first two games, I made some key adjustments that helped us win the next two. One of those adjustments was putting Darrell Armstrong on Tim Hardaway, after Hardaway dropped 20 points on us in Game Two. The result was that Hardaway only scored 12, 16, and 11 points in those final three games.

I also noticed how the Detroit Pistons had played Grant Hill against the Heat, helping him to get into situations where he was isolated, and I applied a few of those same plays to Penny Hardaway. I told Penny what we were doing, and how it had worked for Grant Hill, and I followed that up by telling him, "I think you're better than Grant Hill. I know you think you're better than Grant Hill. I'm giving you these plays. The ball is in your hands." Penny responded by scoring 42 and 41 points in Games Three and Four: the 83 points in two consecutive playoff games is still a franchise record for the Magic. It also marked the first time anyone had ever scored 40-plus points in back-to-back games against a team coached by Pat Riley. It got people's attention. I know it got the Heat's attention.

One of the *Orlando Sentinel* columnists, Brian Schmitz, wrote a column that essentially said I was outcoaching Pat Riley. The headline read: "Riley Can't Compare to Richie and Co.," and the first five paragraphs of Schmitz's column read like this:

> Beetle Bailey is outfoxing Gen. Patton. Street smarts are stumping the NBA's Einstein. Hush Puppies are stepping on Gucci.
>
> Richie Adubato has made Pat Riley's head spin so much the last two games, it's a wonder O-rena fans have not been hit with flying mousse.
>
> Of all the expected mismatches in the Magic-Heat series, none was supposed to be as lopsided as the one involving coaching brain trusts.
>
> Riley had the résumé, the four NBA titles and better hair. But now, as Orlando and Miami head into a decisive Game 5 at Miami Arena on Sunday, it is Richie's Guys who have Riley playing catch-up even with the proceedings tied at 2.
>
> The famed Heat boss of bosses is not only sweating, but Riley may actually have as many hairs out of place on the court as players. And while the Heat starters are being outplayed by the Magic's spare parts, His Highness is being unnerved by the help, the lifelong assistants who make up the Magic's coaching staff.

Penny didn't score 40 points in Game Five, but he did score 33. Without Grant and Seikaly, however, and with Schayes getting into early foul trouble, it wasn't enough, and our season ended in a 91–83 loss. As for the Heat, they went all the way to the Eastern Conference Finals before losing to—who else?—Michael Jordan and the Chicago Bulls.

After that series, Riley made comments to the media, which I really appreciated. He said I made more adjustments and changes than anyone had ever done in any playoff series he coached in. With that endorsement, and with my 64 percent regular-season record, and how well we had played short-handed against the Heat, I really thought I had a chance to be named Orlando's permanent coach. Plus, I had the local media, guys like Brian Schmitz, noting my coaching skills and writing about it.

But the Magic had other ideas. Little did I know that even during the regular season the front office was negotiating hard to bring in Chuck Daly as the next head coach. Chuck was sixty-seven and had been out of the league for three years. But he was also a guy who had won two NBA titles with the "Bad Boy" Detroit Pistons, so his name was always out there whenever there was a coaching vacancy. On top of that, Daly was a Phil-adelphia guy, a former assistant coach with the 76ers, and our front office was loaded with guys with Philadelphia roots—most notably our senior vice president, Pat Williams, and our general manager, John Gabriel.

The Magic dragged out the decision in the off-season. Evi-dently, it was because Daly did not want to return to coaching. But the Magic kept upping the ante. In the meantime, several players came out and publicly endorsed me, including Shaq, who told the *Orlando Sentinel*: "I don't think about the Magic at all. I think about Richie Adubato. I miss him. He was the coolest one. They should keep him. Him and the owner. Every-one else—I have no words for anybody."

My old pal Bob Hill was in the running for the job. He had been fired by the San Antonio Spurs, which a lot of people thought was unfair. In retrospect, the guy who fired him was their general manager and vice president of basketball oper-ations, who then took over the head-coaching reins—Gregg Popovich. Bob called me and asked, "Richie, if I get the job, would you stay on as my assistant?" I thanked him but told him no, that I thought the job should be mine and I would not feel comfortable sticking around in any capacity if the Magic passed on me. Shortly after that conversation, with the Magic dragging their feet, Hill pulled himself out of consideration.

The rumors were flying that Daly was continuing to say no; that he wasn't coming back to coaching. I told my wife, Carol, "It's my job. It's gotta be my job. Chuck Daly obviously doesn't want to coach again and Bobby Hill just pulled himself out of consideration. It's gotta be me."

I felt good. I actually felt elated. I started imagining myself coaching this team at full health. When John Gabriel called me up and asked me to come to his office, I thought for sure they were going to offer me the job. I could not wait to get to his office. Imagine, then, the utter shock I felt when Gabriel looked at me and said, "Richie, we have decided to go with Chuck Daly." My heart dropped. I had waited six weeks for the Magic to make a decision . . . only to be told this. Apparently, Daly's agent, Lonnie Cooper, kept working the Magic until he got Daly a three-year, $15 million contract.

I didn't need to hear anything more. I got up and walked out of Gabriel's office. And then I called my agent. Guess who that was? Lonnie Cooper. My own agent had kept me in the dark, working hard for Chuck Daly to get the job because of the obvious reason that his cut on a $15 million contract was going to be worth a lot more to him than whatever contract the Magic might have offered me. As soon as I could, I called Cooper, cursed him out, and fired him. I also warned him that I never wanted to be in the same room with him again.

I got a phone call from Bob Vander Weide, who at the time was both the team president and owner Rich DeVos's son-in-law. "Richie, I'm sorry," he said. I gave him an earful. "Bob, let me enlighten you," I said. "And I know this for a fact. I don't know what you were looking for, or what you saw, but I know you wanted Chuck Daly all along and I know you want to bring Julius Erving in [which they did, bringing in another Philadelphia guy, in this case naming Dr. J an executive vice president]. I also know you want to bury all the things that have happened here, with Shaq leaving and what Penny and the players did to Brian Hill. I know you think that hiring a guy with a couple of NBA rings is going to generate great press for you guys.

But you should know this: Chuck Daly does not like Penny Hardaway's game. I know this for a fact. He has told people that. He thinks Penny is soft. I have a great relationship with Penny. You're making a big mistake here."

Vander Weide thanked me for that information. He then thought he was going to placate me by saying that he would bring up those concerns with Daly and discuss it with him. "No, don't do that," I said. "Don't do me any favors. This job should have been mine." With that, I hung up.

Just as I had warned them, it never clicked between Daly and Penny. That first year, in 1997–98, the Magic finished .500 with a 41-41 record, fifth in the Atlantic Division, while failing to make the playoffs. The next season, which was truncated because of a lockout, the Magic made the playoffs but lost in four games to—of all teams—the Philadelphia 76ers. Amid growing rumors of tension between him and Penny, Daly quit before the third year of his coaching contract, staying on as a very high-paid consultant.

A month away from sixty-nine years old, Daly announced that he was done for good. "This is a finale for me in coaching," he said. "The mind is willing but the flesh is weak."

True to his word, Daly never coached again in the NBA.

Little did I realize that I also would never be a head coach again in the NBA. But I wasn't done with NBA. And I wasn't finished as a head coach, either.

12

Ricky and Me

To this day I still call Rick Pitino "Ricky." That's because I knew him back in the day—*way* back in the day. We were Hubie Brown's two assistant coaches for the New York Knicks. It was 1983 and Ricky was thirty-one. It was his first pro job of any kind, while I already had been with the team for a year and was a veteran in the league. He was a New York kid and I was a Jersey guy, so we got along great. And we ran together—and I don't mean that we were jogging.

Anytime we won, Ricky and I would go drinking to celebrate, and there were plenty of places to do that in New York City after wins at Madison Square Garden. We had several hangouts where they knew us and treated us well. One night, on an off day after practice, we were at one of our bars, one of our usual hangouts, and they were having some type of costume contest. Keith Hernandez, who at the time was the New York Mets' first baseman, was there, and they corralled the three of us to be judges. It was a crazy fun evening, especially because the drinks were free, and we were throwing 'em back as fast as they could bring 'em.

We got out of there at 3 a.m., and I don't know how Ricky and I got back home to New Jersey, where we were both living—me in West Orange and Ricky in Livingston. But we did. The Knicks had a game later that day, which meant we had to get to the Garden early. When I arrived for all our pregame work, Hubie pulled me aside. "Pitino's real sick," he said. "He's got the flu."

Sick, my ass, I thought. He's hungover.

Hubie added, "You're probably going to have to do his work for him today."

I groaned—although not audibly. While we called Pitino "Ricky" back then, the other moniker we had for him was "Slick Rick"—because he could get his way out of anything. But now he was going to get his way out of a day's work because of being hungover, and needless to say, I wasn't happy.

The one thing about Hubie is that he is a perfectionist, a taskmaster, so doing your own work for him as an assistant coach was nerve-racking enough. But now I was going to have to carry Pitino's load, including all the pregame blackboard work, which I was already dreading. Even though I wasn't as hungover as Ricky was, it wasn't as if I was feeling on top of my game. I went to the nurse's station, where Pitino was. "Ricky, this is bullshit!" I said. "Take a couple of aspirin! Suck it up! I'm not doing your work too!" I probably added a few other choice words for him.

"Okay, I'll try," he said.

For the next two hours, which was mostly spent on the court during the team shootaround and our walkthroughs, I was still doing Pitino's work and mine. By then, I was hoping that at least he would rally in time for the game because I didn't want the burden of being the only assistant coach on the bench feeding Hubie information. If you gave Hubie in-game information or a strategy you thought would work, and it didn't, he would let you know right there courtside—and he would do it with exclamation points and a few well-placed expletives.

A while later, Hubie and I were going over some stuff in his office when, out in the hallway, we saw a nurse pushing Pitino by in a wheelchair toward the exit. Hubie looked at me with sad, sympathetic eyes. "Wow, he's really sick," he said. I wanted to scream: *No, he is not sick! He's hungover!* But I didn't. Instead,

I gave a half-hearted nod and sat there stewing. "Lemme go see if he needs anything," I finally told Hubie, excusing myself as I headed down the hallway. By now, the nurse had pushed Pitino almost to the exit where our staff parking lot was, and I hustled all the way down the hallway.

"Ricky!" I yelled. "You ain't sick! Get back here!"

He never turned around as the nurse kept pushing him in the wheelchair.

"Ricky, you son of a bitch! Don't do this to me! Get your ass back here!"

Pitino jumped out of the wheelchair and sprinted to his parked car. I chased him. But he got to his car before I could get to him, jumped in, and peeled out of the parking lot as I slowed to a sputtering walk, screaming and cursing at him. All I got in return was a lungful of car exhaust and burning rubber.

Hubie was impressed when Pitino made a miraculous recovery and was able to return to the team and his duties the next day—but I wasn't.

I'll say this about Ricky Pitino. He knew his stuff, especially the press-defense. He lived and breathed basketball. We worked well together and continued to run together. Pitino spent two seasons as a Knicks assistant before he went back to the college game, where he had great success at Providence College in Rhode Island.

Pitino came back to become the Knicks' head coach from 1987–89, and when that didn't work out too well he returned to the college game and once again had great success, this time at the University of Kentucky, where he won an NCAA National Championship in 1996.

When Pitino decided to try his coaching whistle again with the NBA, this time in 1997 with the Boston Celtics, he gave me a call shortly after the Orlando Magic let me go. They were giving him anything he wanted in Boston—including a whopping ten-year, $70 million contract. He wanted me to come in as a "consultant" since he didn't have a position on the bench for me—yet. I say yet because he promised me after the first season that he would make it happen, that I would become a full-time assistant, and that the money would be good.

I knew that Ricky, like me, had a defensive mindset, and he could certainly hold his own in drawing up a defensive game plan. But he admitted to me that after failing as a head coach with the Knicks, he thought he needed me to help him with the pro game, especially because the three assistant coaches—Jim O'Brien, John Carroll, and Winston Bennett—were primarily college guys. Ricky liked that I was a veteran NBA coach—someone who had now been a head coach with three teams—and he knew I had my finger on the pulse of what was required to coach a pro player and that I had a real understanding of every aspect of the business. He told me he wanted me, that he *needed* me.

It was all I needed to hear, and I joined Ricky in Boston.

Our families, who already were close, got even closer. Carol and Ricky's wife, Joanne, were always doing things together, and we all often went out to dinner. In every way possible, it was a great fit. I also was obviously happy to not only have another job, but one with an iconic NBA franchise—after all, it doesn't get much better than the Boston Celtics. One problem, though. This wasn't the Celtics of Bob Cousy, Bill Russell, John Havlicek, Dave Cowens, or Larry Bird. These Celtics, going into the 1997–98 season, were coming off what is still the worst record in franchise history, 15-67.

In Pitino's first season, he more than doubled that win total, going 36-46. Things were moving in the right direction. Not that thirty-six victories in eighty-two games is satisfying, but there were two wins from that season that warmed my heart, and both were against my old team—the Orlando Magic. Don't let anyone claim otherwise; when you get fired or told by a team that they no longer want you, you want nothing more than to come back and beat their brains in. I was intricately involved in the game planning against the Magic in those two victories, and when some of Orlando's players saw me pregame they half joked—or maybe not—that they were in trouble, because they knew that I knew them and their game so well.

I was really enjoying myself with the Celtics and looking forward to the off-season, when Pitino was going to follow through and make me a full-fledged assistant—along with the salary it paid—instead of continuing as a consultant.

That off-season, as we were preparing for the NBA Draft, Pitino pulled me aside. "We have the tenth pick in the draft and there is a guy we're thinking of, but I'm getting mixed reports from our scouts. Everyone says he's really good, but soft. Can you look at some tape of him and tell me what you think?" The kid was a guard/forward out of the University of Kansas named Paul Pierce. "Sure," I said.

After watching a lot of tape, I went back to Pitino. "Ricky, let me tell you something. There is no way this kid is soft. No way. I see him physical. I see him diving. I think he's gonna be good. How good? I don't know. But I'm telling you he is not soft."

Pitino really wanted a seven-foot player from Germany named Dirk Nowitzki, and he even flew overseas to see him play. Sitting in the war room on draft day, I was dying. Not because I was worried about recommending Paul Pierce, but because I was sitting next to Red Auerbach, the legendary Celtics head coach and front office executive, who was smoking me out, puffing on cigar after cigar. I hate tobacco smoke. There was some excitement, though, because Nowitzki kept slipping in the draft before he was selected with the ninth pick, just one ahead of us.

So, with the tenth pick, the Boston Celtics took Paul Pierce, who only went on to become a ten-time All-Star with the Celtics, while also helping lead the franchise to an NBA title in 2008.

As for me, I wasn't going to last much longer in Boston.

Pitino was the hottest young head coach in all of basketball, and he was cashing in. He cowrote a book with a *Providence Journal* sports columnist named Bill Reynolds titled *Success Is a Choice: Ten Steps to Overachieving in Business and Life.* That summer of 1998, he was doing a motivational speaking tour promoting the book. One of his tour stops was in Orlando, where I still maintained my home. I went to hear him speak, and in typical Ricky Pitino fashion, he turned it on, mesmerizing the audience. We went back to his hotel suite afterward to talk about my role with the team going forward, and I was expecting him to keep his promise to make me a full assistant with a nice pay increase.

But that wasn't the case.

"Richie," Pitino said, "I can't do it. I've gotta hire a shooting coach."

I knew that, as a team, we shot like crap that previous season, so I got what he was telling me. At the same time, I wasn't getting it. I could feel my Irish Italian anger welling up. The more he talked, trying to explain his way out of the promise he made me, the angrier I got. He might have just mesmerized an entire audience of people, but he wasn't mesmerizing me.

"I'm outta here," I said angrily, bolting out of his hotel room.

"Richie! Richie!" Pitino called after me. "Come back! Let's talk!"

I yelled an expletive at him and kept going. All those years earlier, it was me chasing Pitino into the parking lot at Madison Square Garden. Now it was him chasing me toward the parking lot of an Orlando hotel. When I got outside, I spotted a taxi, jumped in, and told the cabbie to take off right away. He did, with Pitino standing there watching. Maybe Ricky got a lungful of exhaust fumes and a hint of burning rubber. I don't know. All I knew was that once again, I was out of an NBA job—this time for good.

13

I Always Considered Myself a Ladies' Man

I have to admit that when I stormed out of Ricky Pitino's hotel suite, telling him I had quit, I believed I had another job waiting for me. I also knew that after being through so much together and being such good friends, Pitino and I would eventually patch things up—which we did.

On that night when we were both New York Knicks assistant coaches for Hubie Brown and Ricky abandoned me, hungover but claiming he had the flu, I got a lot of help charting plays from Ernie Grunfeld, who was one of the Knicks' bench players. Ernie was a heady player, the kind who you knew would have a career in the game long after his playing days were over.

Sure enough, Ernie worked his way up to president and general manager of the Knicks, and early in 1998, when the Boston Celtics were in New York City for a game, he and I got together for lunch.

I knew that the NBA had expanded into the women's game and started a professional league called the WNBA. Other than being aware of it, I paid little attention to it—that is, until Ernie mentioned it over lunch.

"Richie, what do you think about coaching women?" he asked.

My eyes widened with surprise and then narrowed with curiosity. "I've never coached women before. Why?"

When the WNBA started, franchises were attached to a city where an NBA team was—as a sort of sister team. Ernie was helping run the Liberty, the WNBA's team in New York City.

"Would you be interested in coaching the Liberty?" he asked.

"Ernie, I really don't know anything about the women's game," I said. "It would be a totally new experience."

As we talked, Ernie emphasized that the women's game was fun and that they played hard, fundamental basketball, stressing teamwork and defensive schemes, especially because they didn't play above the basket—or what we call "over the rim"—because the women didn't have the same height and leaping ability as the men.

"You would love it," Ernie said. "And you would be perfect for it."

I did my homework. I talked to several men who had coached women—guys like K. C. Jones, Orlando Woolridge, and Sonny Allen. I reached out to Geno Auriemma, the fantastic women's basketball coach at the University of Connecticut. Everyone I talked to gave me positive feedback, similar to what Ernie was saying. They told me that if I loved to coach fundamental basketball to players who are coachable and who hustle and play with passion, then I would love the WNBA. It intrigued me.

The WNBA was on my mind when I left Pitino's hotel suite. Ernie had been in contact, occasionally inquiring if I was interested in the Liberty's head-coaching job. I was. I felt an undeniable pull. Once you've been a head coach there is always that draw of being a head coach again—especially at a professional level.

The Liberty also played in Madison Square Garden, and for a guy who grew up in Jersey, going to the Garden is like Mecca. I never tired of walking onto the court at the Garden; the feeling was always exhilarating. In fact, the first time I did, as a Knicks assistant coach, I walked to center court, knelt, and said a prayer.

There were other factors playing on my mind. My father, Adam Adubato, was living in Ocean Gate, New Jersey, and he was up in years and bedridden. I wanted to be there for him because my dad was always there for me.

I loved my dad, and I knew my love of sports came from him.

When I was kid, my father owned an Esso gas station in Millburn, New Jersey, with four service bays and mechanics; but he still was at every one of my games. He never missed. Baseball, basketball . . . whatever it was, he was there. I also grew up working at my father's station—pumping gas, checking the oil, washing windows, Simonizing cars, and basically doing anything needed that didn't require me putting a tool in my hands. I was surrounded by great mechanics, and I knew I wasn't destined to be one of them. I knew sports were my future, and baseball easily could have been where I headed. My dad, after all, was a big baseball guy who once owned and managed a semi-pro team named the East Orange Soverels. He was also a scout for the Cincinnati Reds and Boston Red Sox.

When I was eight years old, we moved from Newark to East Orange. Looking back, I can see what a blessing that was. Newark was divided into wards based on ethnicity, and the inner-city school system had its normal host of problems. At East Orange, the education was much better, and the parks and recreation programs were considered to be the best in the northeast. Locally, Panzer College was where guys went to become physical education teachers. They became our coaches, and in the summer they ran the parks and all the sports leagues and programs. You name it, we played it. Not only did I get a well-rounded sports background, but I received great coaching, while also playing sports with kids from other ethnic backgrounds, including the black kids. It was a great way to grow up, and I learned a lot of life lessons that remain with me today.

I became good enough at baseball to become a college player and even get a tryout with the Philadelphia Phillies. But of all the sports, basketball was my passion, and eventually my direction veered toward coaching hoops.

For those, and so many other reasons, I always felt fondly rooted to New Jersey. So when Ernie Grunfeld called again and offered me the Liberty head-coaching job, I took it and moved back to the northeast and began preparing for the 1999 WNBA season. When I got to the WNBA and the Liberty, I soon learned that it was a whole new ballgame. It was still pro basketball. The basics were the same. They played on the same-sized courts, in the same buildings, by the same rules, under rims that were ten feet off the ground . . . but, then again, it was *different*.

I became acutely aware of that the first time I had to cut players. In this case I had to cut fifteen players down to twelve. There is no coach who relishes cutting players. Every coach hates doing it. It's one of the most difficult things to do. Cutting a player might mean the end of their career, and no coach wants to be the bearer of that kind of bad news.

I brought the first two ladies into my office and told them they did not make the team. Then I did what a coach in that position always tries to do, which is tell them that their career does not have to be over. "You might look into playing in Europe," I said. "Keep working hard. This doesn't need to be the end of the road."

One of the players immediately started crying, and the other started bawling, her body heaving in convulsions. I stood there stunned, not knowing what to do. When you cut men from an NBA team, they don't start crying. They curse you and threaten to punch you out. Not all of them, but some of them. What they don't do is cry—at least not in front of you. But here I had two women in front of me, one crying, the other bawling. And I still had one more player to cut.

Carol Blazejowski was our general manager and also a former pro player. We called her Blaze. I went to her office. "Blaze," I said, "I just cut two players, and they're both in my office crying their eyes out. I have one more to cut. I'm not cutting three in one day and going through that again. It's too hard. So you can cut the third player if you want. But I'm not doing it. I'll keep her and give her a uniform and find a way to keep thirteen."

Well, Blaze was used to this. She had cut female players before, so she went and took care of business.

Here was another difference I soon learned. Everything would be going well. We would be having good practices. And then all of a sudden, one, two, three, or more of the players would be extremely irritable. This struck me one day when one of my favorite players, Kym Hampton, suddenly turned into someone I didn't recognize. During a practice I told Kym, "When you cut across into the post you have to fake first and go a little faster." Kym whirled around and with a cross look said, "I can't satisfy you at all today, can I?" It took me aback. And then it clicked. I'm no genius, but I instantly realized it was that time of the month. Kym was having her period. What baffled me, though, was that a lot of the other players, who were normally just fabulous to coach, were just as cranky.

I talked to our head trainer, Lisa White, and asked her what in the heck was going on. She explained to me a phenomenon I wasn't aware of, but it apparently was well known—that when a group of women get together, whether it's basketball, softball, a dorm room, whatever, they tend to eventually get their monthly periods at the same time. I actually called around and checked with other people who coached women and got the same message.

I went back to Lisa. "I need you to monitor this for me," I said. If we were walking out to practice and she held up eight fingers, or nine or ten, I would turn to the players and say, "Ladies, go to lunch today. Relax. No practice. Just shoot foul shots and leave. I'll see you tomorrow."

That didn't happen often, maybe once or twice a season. But it did happen, and I wasn't going to go through a two-hour practice trying to accomplish what I wanted to under those conditions. A little different from men? Yes. But you adjust.

One particular night, I had a player—a foreign player who was an excellent shooter—and she came out on fire. We were playing at the Garden, and she came off the bench and hit four jumpers in a row to ignite us. The next thing I knew, my trainer Lisa was in my ear.

"Richie, you gotta get her out right now," she said.

"Get her out? Why would I get her out? She just made four jumpers! I'm calling two more plays for her!"

"She's got a real problem, and if you don't get her out it could be embarrassing."

"Okay, okay," I said. "I'll get her out, but let me call two quick plays."

I did, and we scored a couple of more times. And then I noticed blood on her uniform, and I felt horrible. I quickly called a timeout. I told Lisa and our assistant trainer to please run out and help her to the locker room. Again, you adjust. You learn and adjust.

Overall, I loved coaching women. Absolutely loved it. As a coach you enjoy working with players who are eager to learn and who work hard at their game. In that regard, I think women are better than men. And women play a very physical brand of basketball. Don't let anyone tell you otherwise. I was stunned when I saw Teresa Weatherspoon, who played for us, go against the Utah Starzz's Debbie Black. I thought I was watching a mixed martial arts bout instead of basketball. For forty minutes they guarded each other for all ninety-four feet—pressuring each other from baseline to baseline. They collided constantly, but neither backed down. They were guarding each other so closely it was as if they were in each other's uniforms—when one breathed in the other breathed out. Elbows and punches flew on a regular basis. One time, when none of the officials were looking, 'Spoon, as we called Weatherspoon, punched Black right in the forehead, knocking her down. Black bounced right back up and continued guarding 'Spoon. All I could do is shake my head. You don't see that in the men's game. It was impressive.

Again, however, you adjust to that.

Lisa Leslie was one of the best WNBA players of all time, leading the Los Angeles Sparks to two WNBA Championships in 2001 and 2002. She was also one of the league's most aggressive and physical players. Leslie was always throwing elbows under the basket while battling for rebounds from the center position. I pulled my centers aside. "Don't let Leslie get away with that," I said. I knew from the men's game that if you backed down from a physical player, the onslaught would continue. They wouldn't listen, though. So I kept after them. "Elbow her back!" I said. "Don't let her continue to beat you like that." Finally, I got through to them and they began retaliating. It worked. Leslie started backing off a bit.

The one constant—always—is that this was basketball; the game I had spent all my life involved with. I knew I could coach, and coach I did. We had a talented team and they responded to me, which was great. In my first season with that 1999 Liberty team we won the Eastern Conference and beat the Charlotte Sting 2–1 in a three-game series to advance to the WNBA Finals against the powerhouse Houston Comets in what would also be a three-game series. The Comets, led by the terrific Sheryl Swoopes, Tina Thompson, and Cynthia Cooper, won the first game, 73–60, at the Garden, with the next two games scheduled to be played at Houston's Compaq Center—if it went to the full three games.

And it did.

For my money, Game Two was the greatest WNBA game ever played. But I admit to being a little biased. I was also a little scared after we fell behind 37–23 in the first half, and at one point we were down by 18. But we only shot 30 percent, and I knew we were too good to keep shooting that bad. But the hometown Houston fans were raucous, trying to rattle my players, and I kept imploring them to stay calm, stay within themselves, play their game. When we came out the second half, we were both calm and fired up. Steadily, we closed the gap and it seemed to rattle the Comets, who only shot 21 percent in the second half to our 44 percent. It helped that we were playing great defense—my specialty. I made some adjustments with our schemes at halftime.

With 1:20 remaining we had taken a 63–62 lead as I paced the sideline. But the Comets sank a bucket, got a steal, were fouled, and their forward Tina Thompson went to the free-throw line, where she missed the first shot and made the second. Down 65–63 with 28.4 seconds left, I called timeout. We brought the ball up court, fought through their defense, and got Crystal Robinson free enough to sink a shot just in front of the three-point line to tie the game at 65. It was short-lived, however, because Tina Thompson banked a shot in from the baseline to put the Comets up, 67–65, with just 2.4 seconds remaining.

We had no timeouts left. All I could do was stand on the sidelines, helpless. Teresa Weatherspoon got the inbounds pass from Kym Hampton just as celebratory confetti started falling from the rafters. The Comets jumped the gun, convinced that they had won the WNBA title. But 'Spoon dribbled twice while running, trying to shake off a lone defender. Just behind midcourt she threw up a prayer. It was answered. It was a rainbow of a shot that found its pot of gold at the bottom of the net, but not before it banked off the backboard, giving us a 68–67 win. I was stunned, but not as stunned as the sixteen thousand-plus people at the Compaq Center. The confetti continued to fall. As the players mobbed each other at center court it seemed as if we had won the WNBA title. But we hadn't. There was one more game to play, and we lost that one to a very, very good Comets team, 59–47.

Houston had been the dominant team that whole regular season, going 26-6. Led by those three terrific All-Star caliber players—Swoopes, Thompson, and Cooper—it was also the third of four consecutive WNBA titles for the Comets. In fact, it was also the first four years of the league's existence. As for me, it was quite a first year. A fun year. What a great game and league. Whatever reservations I had coming into the WNBA were way behind me, and I was looking forward to the future.

14

Finishing in a Blaze . . . but Not of Glory

We didn't have many perks in the WNBA. Unlike the NBA, we didn't travel on private planes or stay in fancy hotels. We flew coach on commercial flights and stayed in run-of-the-mill hotels. But one thing I did enjoy was that the women were very coachable and they left it all on the court every game—they ran, played defense, rebounded, and hustled. What more could I ask for? The other thing I enjoyed about the WNBA was that you recruited players. Because basketball is an international sport, we recruited players from overseas. Every off-season, I visited beautiful towns all over Europe in countries like Italy, France, the Czech Republic, Belgium, Germany, and Poland, trying to convince some of the top European athletes to come play for the New York Liberty. It helped that I was recruiting not to a college campus but to the greatest city in the world.

One player I really wanted to bring to the Liberty was a Polish center named Margo Dydek. She was seven feet two. I saw her play in a tournament in Poland and she was a force under the basket. After the game, she walked out of her team's locker room wearing high heels—standing about seven and a half feet tall in them. What a sight! And what a personality she had, too. Craning my neck as I looked up, I talked to Margo about her game. Her head was practically touching the ceiling. She was easy to talk to, and she spoke about a half dozen languages, so I kidded with her, speaking in the only language I knew—Jersey.

"Margo, how are you ever gonna meet a man?" I asked.

"Coach, maybe I need two!" she replied, a twinkle in her eye.

I laughed. I told her, perhaps only half jokingly, that I wanted to hook her up with Marcin Gortat, the six-foot-eleven center for the Orlando Magic, who was also Polish. I wanted them to get married, and then I'd be the agent for all the kids they would have.

Sadly, Margo Dydek never played for us. Instead, she played for the WNBA's Utah Starzz, the San Antonio Silver Stars, the Connecticut Sun, and the Los Angeles Sparks. She also married a gentleman named David Twigg and they had two sons. After her playing career was over, Margo got into coaching, and in 2011 she was an assistant coach in Brisbane, Australia, for the Northside Wizards in the Queensland Basketball League. While she was coaching there, Margo suffered a massive heart attack. Eight days later she and her unborn baby both died. Margo Dydek was only thirty-seven.

News of her death shook me. But if not for coaching in the WNBA I never would have met her, gotten to know her, and competed against her. I was meeting so many great people in the WNBA. The league opened the door to a whole new world of basketball, and I loved it.

Another player I tried to recruit was a Russian named Elena Baranova. She had played for the WNBA's Utah Starzz and Miami Sol, but she was now back home in Russia, where I happened to be doing some coaching in the off-season. Baranova was six feet five, a terrific player, and she wanted to return to the WNBA. I wanted her on the Liberty in the worst way. My agent, Bruce Levy, was with me in Russia, and we went together to meet with Elena and her husband at her parents' house. It was a modest house, which is fairly standard for most Russian homes. The other standard is that everybody there drinks vodka. It's everywhere—and I do mean everywhere. You can even buy vodka from vending machines. I swear they must breastfeed their children on vodka. The other staple is caviar. Vodka, I can handle; caviar, not so much. I'm a Jersey guy. We don't eat fish eggs. I had heard, however, that if you do eat caviar, the best are the ones that have reddish dots in them.

Sure enough, when we were all sitting around at Baranova's parents' home, out came the drinks and appetizers—vodka and caviar. When Elena's father, who spoke broken English, put the caviar on the table, I noticed the reddish dots. I still couldn't bring myself to eat any. Then he poured me some vodka . . . and poured and poured and poured. It seemed as if he poured a half pitcher of vodka into my glass straight up on the rocks. I turned to Elena and asked, "Do you have any orange juice?" "Sure, coach," she said, getting up. "I'll get you some." As she disappeared into the kitchen, I caught her father out of the corner of my eye scrunching his face with displeasure, as if he had just bitten into a lemon. That worried me. I didn't want anything to happen that might prevent this fabulous player from coming to New York and playing for the Liberty. "You know what, Elena?" I called out. "I'll drink the vodka like this."

A few moments later, I excused myself to use the bathroom. As I did I leaned into my agent's ear and whispered, "Bruce, I'll be back in a moment. Eat my caviar for me." When I came back the caviar was gone, but Elena's father was ready to pour another huge glass of vodka for me. Since I had already drunk one full glass and could feel the effects starting to swirl in my head, I asked Elena to fill half the glass with orange juice this time.

All in all, the recruiting visit went very well, and Elena Baranova came to New York City and became a very productive player for the Liberty. Oh, and I still drink my vodka with orange juice. I also still don't eat caviar—reddish dots or not.

In the early years of the WNBA, the NBA really promoted and marketed it, which brought us a lot of attention. One day before a game at Madison Square Garden, I ran into Reggie

Miller, who was that skinny kid I first met when he played for UCLA and later tormented me as a future Hall of Fame player for the Indiana Pacers. Reggie was on the sideline watching our pregame shootaround. Becky Hammon, our terrific point guard, had a ritual at the end of every shootaround; she would take ten shots from half court before she left the gym. It gave me an idea to have a little fun with Reggie, who always fancied himself as the best shooter around.

"Hey Reggie," I said, pointing to Hammon. "See that woman over there? She's a better shooter than you are. You know that, right?"

Reggie laughed.

"No, no, I'm serious," I said. "She's better than you."

He kept laughing.

"Tell you what," I said. "I've got two hundred-dollar bills in my wallet that say she can outshoot you. I'll put them right here on the table. She'll take five shots from half court. You take five, and we'll see who wins."

As I laid the two one-hundred-dollar bills on the table, Reggie's laugh turned into a big grin. He also had two one-hundred-dollar bills in his wallet, and he couldn't get to half court fast enough. Back and forth Becky and Reggie went, shooting from half court. Sure enough, Becky sank two and Reggie only one. As I collected two one-hundred-dollar bills from him, I gave one of them to Becky and kept the other for myself. Then I told Reggie, "Don't worry, Reggie, I won't say that one of the best shooters of all time got beat by a woman." However, I didn't promise Reggie that I would not write about it—in a book.

Reggie has nothing to be embarrassed about, though. Hammon was special, and not just at shooting. After her playing career ended in 2012, Becky became a full-time assistant coach with the NBA's San Antonio Spurs in 2014. In doing so, she also became the first full-time female assistant coach in any of the four major professional sports leagues in America—MLB, NHL, NFL, and NBA. In 2015, she also became the head coach in the Spurs' Summer League—the first woman to accomplish that, too.

I have been thrilled to see Becky Hammon forging her way into the NBA because men have certainly enjoyed being in the WNBA. Aside from me, there were several other men coaching in the WNBA—some I liked, and others not so much. Falling into that latter category was Bill Laimbeer. In his playing days, Laimbeer was known as probably the baddest of the "Bad Boy" Detroit Pistons—just an unlikable, dirty player.

He also was, in my opinion, the all-time greatest flopper in NBA history. He had an uncanny ability to get a foul called on the other guy. He could make the slightest nudge seem like he was getting mugged. If there was an Academy Award given for that type of acting on a basketball court, Laimbeer would have won it every year. Guys hated him.

I coached against Laimbeer in the WNBA, and I tried to follow the unwritten protocol of postgame sportsmanship, which I admittedly have mixed emotions about. After losing a fiercely competitive game I am in no mood to walk over and shake the other coach's hand. I think a simple wave is good enough. Maybe a wave and a head nod, and then adjourn to your respective locker rooms. But in the WNBA, it isn't like that. In the WNBA everyone comes across the floor after games and shakes hands, and some even hug.

Once, after we beat the Detroit Shock, who were coached by Laimbeer, I went over to shake his hand. As I did, Laimbeer leaned into me, and with that deadpan look of his, he said, "Richie, sorry we didn't show up tonight." I felt my Irish Italian ire rise in me. Saying *we didn't show up* is about as backhanded a compliment as you can get, and Laimbeer knew it. Not that he cared. That's Laimbeer—a jerk. I was ready for him the next time we beat them. Before he could get a word out, I looked him in the eye, and with a smile that was more like a smirk, I said, "Hey Bill, this is the second time your team didn't show up against us. You better start coaching 'em better."

Another former Detroit Piston bad boy, Rick Mahorn, was

Laimbeer's assistant coach, and he heard what I said. Later, after the game, I ran into Mahorn, and he said to me, laughing, "Richie, man, you really got Laimbeer with that one." I smiled and said, "You didn't think I was going to let him give me one of his backhanded compliments again, did you?"

Meanwhile, I was having success coaching the Liberty:

In 1999 we went to the WNBA Finals.

In 2000 we went to the WNBA Finals.

In 2001 we went to the WNBA Eastern Conference Finals.

In 2002 we went to the WNBA Finals.

But in 2003 we missed the postseason because of an odd turn of events:

The team was scheduled to play a game on August 14, 2003, and we were at Madison Square Garden, warming up for the game, when the lights went out, completely out—and stayed out. We soon learned that it wasn't just us who were without electricity. It was millions of people across several states and two countries in what came to be known as the Northeast blackout of 2003. Our game was canceled, and my assistant coaches, some of the players, and I walked across the street to the hotel where we were living. I was staying on the twenty-eighth floor, while my assistant coaches and some of the players were on the twenty-fifth floor.

I was sixty-five years old at the time, and I considered myself in good shape. Obviously, without any electricity the elevators were not operating, so we started walking the stairs. We climbed . . . and climbed and climbed and climbed. It seemed to never end. I thought I was climbing Mount Everest. At the twentieth floor we stopped, sat down, and caught our breath. Without any air conditioning running, and it being mid-August, we were all drenched with sweat. When we got to the twenty-fifth floor, one of my young assistant coaches, Jeff House, turned to me and asked if I wanted him to walk me up the last three floors. "I-I'm f-fine, I-I'll be o-o-okay," I said, panting for air.

I allowed myself to catch my breath before continuing. "But if I don't call you in ten minutes that means I didn't make it. You'll know I had a heart attack or stroke. So if I don't call, come looking for me." Those last three flights were like reaching the peak of a mountain, but I made it. I would never want to have to do that again.

The blackout ended, but it was only the beginning of the effect it had on us. It really screwed up our schedule. In our last six games we had to play three games in a row, and then our last three games in four days. We went 3-3 in those six games, finished the season 16-18 and missed the postseason for the first time in my head-coaching tenure there. Little did I realize that it would be my last full season coaching the Liberty.

I pride myself in getting along with people, but unfortunately, toward the end of my six-year run with the Liberty I started butting heads with our general manager Carol Blazejowski, whom we called Blaze. Blaze was a Jersey girl, though not the type that Bruce Springsteen sings about. I first became aware of her when she was a prep star at Cranford High School in New Jersey and later a collegiate standout at Montclair State, which is also in New Jersey. She was an electric college player—her claim to fame was scoring 52 points in a college game at Madison Square Garden, still the most ever by either a man or a woman.

I sensed that the 2004 season was going to be a challenge. When we got an advanced copy of the schedule, I saw that eleven of our first sixteen games were on the road. That's a killer way to start any season, and especially so when you're only playing thirty-four games. I asked Blaze if she could look into maybe getting one or two of our road games switched to a home game and balance out the schedule that way. She wouldn't do it.

Early in the season, Blaze suspended one of our forward-centers, Tari Phillips. She had wanted to trade Tari before the season began, but I wouldn't let her unless she could get a comparable center in return, and evidently Blaze could not. Tari was sometimes a pain to deal with, I'll admit that. She would show up for a road game, sometimes late, with five suitcases. One time she got on the wrong train when we were going to Washington DC to play the Mystics. She was also known to run up phone bills from the hotel, sometimes over a $1,000. Tari was unconventional, to say the least, but we worked around it. Besides, when I was with the Magic, I had known Tari from when she played at Edgewater High School and the University of Central Florida—both in Orlando. She used to come to our games. I liked her and I could coach her, and she gave it her all on the court. She could go toe-to-toe with some of those tough, physical centers around the league. But against my wishes, Blaze suspended her for those first eight games. We also missed Crystal Robinson, our go-to clutch shooter, the last three games with an injury. So now we were playing eleven of our first sixteen games on the road—the first eight without our center. It was a recipe for disaster.

The worst thing to happen at the start of the season was not getting a point guard we desperately needed. I was talking to my buddy Dick Vitale, who would work basketball camps at the famous IMG Academy in Bradenton, Florida, near where he lived. He told me about a player named Niesha Butler who had played at IMG and was good enough to be recruited by the two best college women's programs in the country—Tennessee and Connecticut. She played at Georgia Tech and then left basketball to pursue acting and modeling in Los Angeles. But now, Vitale told me, she was ready to return to basketball, and he assured me that she was a great point guard.

I called Blaze and told her about Niesha Butler and asked if we could bring her into camp. Her response indicated that she was already well aware of Niesha.

"We will never bring her into camp," Blaze said flatly.

Her response stunned me. "Why not?" I asked.

"We would just never bring her here."

I asked my two assistant coaches, Patty Coyle and Jeff House, if they had heard of her. Not only had they heard of her, they also gave her glowing reports. I asked Blaze again, telling her that Patty and Jeff said she was a terrific player. The three of us even met with Blaze just before training camp began, and we all told her we wanted to bring Niesha in. Blaze reluctantly conceded.

I brought her in, and I was glad I did. She could play a solid point guard and was an answer to what we were looking for. When it came time during training camp to make our first round of cuts, the four of us—Blaze, Coyle, House, and I—met as we normally did. If the vote was tied at 2–2, I had the deciding vote as the head coach. When Niesha Butler's name was discussed, the vote was 3–1 to keep her on the roster, with Blaze casting the only dissenting vote. Two things were obvious: Niesha had the skills to be a very good starting point guard for us, and yet for some unreasonable reason Blaze did not even want her on the roster.

After one more week of practice, we needed to make our final cuts down to twelve roster spots. By now, Niesha was playing exceptionally well. Blaze intercepted me before the four of us went into a meeting. "Richie," she said. "I didn't like the way the last meeting went. I just want you and me to make the final decisions on the cuts." I was a bit taken aback, but I nodded and shrugged. "By the way, don't worry about making a decision on Niesha. I already cut her and sent her home."

I lost it. I couldn't believe what I was hearing. Why? I kept wondering. Was there some other motive I wasn't aware of? All that mattered to me was that we needed a point guard, and Niesha was really, really good.

"You know, Blaze," I said, my voice rising in anger. "I've worked for a lot of organizations with a lot of general managers. You've got the biggest ego of anybody I've ever known."

I expected her to take a swing at me. I really did. Instead, she ran out of the room crying.

I knew my days were numbered.

We went on that brutal road trip and finished 7-9, which I was actually happy about, even though we had just lost eight of our last nine. The good news was that we were only a game and a half out of first place. Back in New York, we were scheduled to play in a makeshift basketball arena at Radio City Music Hall because Madison Square Garden was going to be used for the 2004 Republican National Convention. I was happy about that, too. I had played in funky settings like that before in college, against Long Island University and Glassboro State College, where the court is a stage, almost like the fans are watching a play or a concert instead of a basketball game. The home team gets used to it, but it's very disconcerting for the visiting team. It's a tremendous home-court advantage.

"We're 7-9, but we're only a game and a half out of first place and most of our remaining games are at home," I told our players after our final road game in Sacramento. "We're gonna play most of our remaining games at Radio City Music Hall, and we're gonna finish strong."

When we got back to New York, Blaze called me at the airport and said she wanted to see me at seven o'clock the next morning. When we met, she fired me.

My wife, Carol, and I went to a bar that night, and while we were sitting there watching ESPN, feeling pretty bad, a ticker scrolled across the bottom of the TV screen. It said:

Richie Adubato fired today by New York Liberty. Adubato the only coach to be fired by both the NBA and WNBA.

Ouch! They could have said I was the only coach to have led both an NBA *and* a WNBA team to the playoffs. But they didn't. Or they could have said that I was the only coach to have won at least one hundred games as a head coach in both the NBA and WNBA. But they didn't. Of course not.

I'm not going to minimize how much that hurt. It did. A lot. I loved coaching the Liberty and coaching at Madison Square Garden, where I spent nine years coaching—five years with the Liberty and four years as a Knicks assistant coach. Those nine years were some of the best years of my life. Growing up in New Jersey, I went to Madison Square Garden many times as a fan. I was even there, sitting in the stands, the night that Knicks center Willis Reed dramatically hobbled onto the court in Game Seven of the 1970 NBA Finals against the Los Angeles Lakers. Reed scored New York's first two baskets en route to the Knicks winning that game and the Finals. That was, and still is, the loudest I have ever heard a crowd at Madison Square Garden—just deafening.

In five full seasons as the Liberty's head coach, we had gone to the WNBA Finals three times and the Eastern Conference Finals once. The Liberty has yet to win an Eastern Conference Finals since then, much less make it back to the WNBA Finals. To this day, whenever I'm at Madison Square Garden, I take a moment to look up at the rafters. I specifically gaze at three championship banners from when I coached the team in 1999, 2000, and 2002. Ever since Blaze fired me, they haven't won a championship of any kind. They got close in 2015, when the Liberty made it to the third and final game of the Eastern Conference Finals against the Indiana Fever. I was at a sports bar near where I live in Orlando, watching that deciding Game Three, and I'll admit that I was rooting like crazy for the Fever. I had nothing against the Liberty. I really didn't care if they won or lost. But I didn't want their coach to win. You see, their coach now was Bill Laimbeer.

Needless to say, I was thrilled when the Fever beat Laimbeer's Liberty team, 66–51. To celebrate, I ordered champagne for the whole bar.

15

Into the Mystic

I wasn't out of a job long, which was good. I like to work. I like to coach. In 2005, the Washington Mystics were an average WNBA franchise—at best. In their seven years of existence, the Mystics had compiled an 82-144 record. Okay, maybe they weren't average. They had also been through seven head coaches. I became their eighth.

The cornerstone of the Mystics' franchise had been Chamique Holdsclaw, a six-foot-two forward who could score and do it all. Holdsclaw was a former first-round pick out of the University of Tennessee, where she helped Coach Pat Summitt win three consecutive NCAA National Championships. She was a player. But during the 2004 season, Holdsclaw went a bit AWOL, disappearing from the team for eleven games and also for the playoffs. She later said it was because of depression.

I would like to have coached Holdsclaw, but I never got the chance. The Mystics traded her on March 21, 2005, sending her to the Los Angeles Sparks for DeLisha Milton-Jones and a first-round draft pick. Milton-Jones was a solid player, a six-foot-one forward, but she was no Holdsclaw.

It was a month after that trade, on April 21, 2005, when I was hired to be the Mystics' head coach.

The Washington DC–area media trumpeted my hiring, noting that I was the third coach in WNBA history to reach one hundred victories. The Mystics released a statement from Pat Summitt, who served as a personnel consultant to the team, in which she said, "I can't imagine us getting someone that has more experience and success than Richie. We are excited to have him in place, and we are anxious to get started."

By now I was used to coaching the women's game, and problem players never flustered me. People are people, and in the coaching profession you come across all sorts of personalities— male and female—and you learn how to deal with them, especially if they are star players. Generally, though, I found WNBA players to be much more attentive in team meetings than NBA players. But, as always, there are exceptions.

The two players I had with the Mystics who could be a real pain were Chasity Melvin and Nikki Teasley. Chasity was our center and a star player. Nikki was an okay point guard, nothing special. I inherited Chasity when I became coach; Nikki came my second year.

Nikki was always just in time, or late, for our film sessions. All the chairs were classroom-type folding chairs, but there was one chair that was cushioned, and Nikki immediately staked claim on that chair as hers. That wasn't too annoying, except that she would lean back in the chair and never look at the film. She wasn't exactly asleep, but she certainly wasn't paying attention. She did other things that annoyed me, like the time when I noticed that during a game the women went from playing zone to man-to-man defense, and it cost us a few quick baskets. I called a timeout and asked what was going on, and the girls told me that Nikki said we needed to switch from zone to man-to-man. "Oh, so Nikki is now the coach!" I bellowed. I was furious. We also ended up losing the game, which didn't help my mood.

It finally got to me that Nikki insisted on sitting on the cushioned chair during our film sessions and then wouldn't pay attention. I'd get on her about it, but nothing seemed to faze her. I knew about a section in our arena where parents could bring their little children—a sort of a kindergarten area, with highchairs. One day, I slipped the janitor ten bucks and asked him to remove the comfortable cushioned chair from our film room and replace it with one of the highchairs. "Bring me a little plate of the cookies too," I said.

The next time we had a film session, everyone was there a little early. As usual, Nikki walked in just in time. When she looked over to where her cushioned chair always was, she saw the highchair. "I thought you'd like the highchair if you're gonna act like a baby," I said. Then I pointed to the plate of cookies. "And over there are some cookies in case you get hungry." The team burst out laughing. Nikki was upset. But I think she was more embarrassed than upset. And she got the point.

Problem players are one thing to deal with. Problem management is entirely different. A few weeks after I was hired, Abe Pollin and his Washington Sports & Entertainment group sold the Mystics to Lincoln Holdings LLC, with Sheila Johnson named as a part-owner/partner. It made history because Johnson became the WNBA's first black female owner, with the titles of president, managing partner, and governor. Sheila and her ex-husband, Bob Johnson, who became America's first black billionaire, had cofounded the entertainment network BET. They had also owned the NBA's Charlotte Bobcats. Sheila had money. Lots of money. I found her to be a lovely woman and I liked her a lot. I also liked that she was a smart businesswoman with a deep pocketbook. But being smart in business and being smart in basketball are two different things.

Sheila made her right-hand man a guy named Curtis Symonds, whose basketball background was coaching at the AAU level. His working background, and it was a successful one, was in cable television, specifically in sales and marketing with the BET brand. Sheila gave Curtis some type of consultant title with the Mystics, and it wasn't long before he and I were butting heads. It wasn't that Curtis thought he knew more about basketball than I did. It was more than that. Curtis was one of those guys who thought he invented the game.

Once, during an exhibition game, Curtis questioned me about the pick-and-roll. It wasn't so much a question as it was a challenge, a sort of indictment on my coaching knowledge. But I played along with him and invited him into my office. Over the next hour I showed him on the blackboard thirteen ways to execute the pick-and-roll, breaking it down into all its minute details. The nonverbal message was, You want to question my coaching knowledge? Well here is my coaching knowledge. You would think he'd get the point, but arrogant people rarely do.

We went 16-18 that 2005 season, missing the playoffs, but I knew we were building. My second year we turned in a winning record, going 18-16 and making the playoffs, losing to Connecticut in the Eastern Conference Semifinals. Still, it was an improvement over my first season coaching the team, and I was looking forward to more improvements.

Eventually, Chasity Melvin's antics wore on Curtis and our general manager, Linda Hargrove, and they wanted to trade her. Chasity could match Curtis with her arrogance. She always thought she knew better than anyone else. I could handle her, though. It helped that we had the same agent, Bruce Levy. I'd call Bruce and tell him to talk to Chasity, which he would do, telling her that I was going to make her a better player. And, as any professional athlete can tell you, being a better player means making better money. So even though Chasity was a problem, I had no problem with her. You work around your star players, and she was a star for us.

But Curtis and Linda kept talking to me about trading her for a small forward who had played at Duke and who was a good player—good, but not Chasity Melvin. I told them no way. We needed Chasity at center, and if we traded her for a small forward it would create a hole in the middle of our starting five. I thought we had a chance to win the Eastern Conference that 2007 season, and I knew Chasity was going to be an important piece on our team if we were going to do that. But Curtis had it in his head that Chasity needed to be traded. I could understand Curtis having faulty judgment, so when his thinking on personnel matters was off base it didn't surprise me. But the fact that Linda wanted to trade Chasity concerned me, because Linda knew her stuff. Before she became our GM, Linda had coached the Portland franchise. She was also a wonderful person. She was the one who hired me, so I had extra reason to like her. Whereas Curtis didn't know what he was talking about, I think Linda was just fed up with Chasity.

One day, when Curtis again broached the subject of trading Chasity, I flat told him, "Listen, if you don't want to win this year, or if you just want to barely make the playoffs, then go ahead and make this trade." Curtis argued that our backup center was just as good. She wasn't.

We started the season 0-2, and I was frustrated. Our next game was against the New York Liberty, and as always, I wanted to beat them in the worst way. In our hotel late that night before the game, my assistant coaches, Linda, Curtis, and I had a meeting, and once again the subject of trading Chasity came up. We agreed to shelve the idea for now and discuss it again when we got back to Washington.

I didn't sleep well, turning over in my mind all the reasons why it would be dumb to trade Chasity. The next morning I rode the team bus to Madison Square Garden. Curtis rode with us, and I couldn't wait to get off and again go over all my concerns with him. I reiterated that if we traded her we wouldn't make the playoffs, that our backup center wasn't as good, and that if we promoted the backup center it would leave us without a backup to her. Curtis listened and nodded to everything I said. When I finished he gave me one final nod, said, "Okay," and walked away.

Once inside, I got our team together in the locker room and started to go over our game plan and each player's matchups and assignments. "Now Chasity," I began, "you've got—"

Several players immediately interrupted me.

"Coach, Chasity's not here. She's been traded."

I felt my face redden from both embarrassment and anger.

Especially anger. Curtis and Linda had engineered a trade either that morning or the night before and never told me. Making matters worse, we lost to the Liberty that night. I knew if we still had Chasity we would have won that game. I was out of my mind with frustration and anger.

On the train ride back to Washington, I heard somebody mention that we were 0-3. "No!" I barked. "We're 0-2! I'm not taking that loss! They can't take my starting center away from me and not even give me a practice to prepare for my next game and then tell me we lost that game! No way!"

If Curtis was going to trade my starting center out from under me, then I figured I should get something in return. Our next game was against the Detroit Shock. We had a couple of practices, but because I was still stewing, it was hard for me to concentrate. The day before the game, I called Curtis.

"Look, you made it very, very difficult for us by making that trade," I told him. "Now we probably won't make the playoffs. You've put me in a hole and I don't want that on me. I want a new contract. I want some security because of what happened. I think you guys should give me a two-year extension, because this whole situation is really ridiculous."

Needless to say, I didn't get a contract extension. I think Sheila Johnson wanted to give me a new contract, but she didn't have total authority. When I heard back from Curtis, he told me they didn't give contracts in the middle of a season. We played the Shock in Detroit and lost by 15 points. Now we were 0-4, but I was convinced we would have been 2-2 if we still had Chasity. So I did what in my heart I believed I had to do—I resigned. It was the first time in my career I had ever done that. But I was so infuriated and embarrassed that I really didn't think I had a choice. I later realized it was one of the dumbest things I ever did. Why? Because when you quit you don't get paid. You should always let them fire you instead.

One of my assistant coaches, Tree Rollins, took over, and the next game was against the Chicago Sky, the team the Mystics had traded Chasity to. Not surprisingly, Chasity led the Sky to a 75–70 victory against her former team. No offense to Tree, but just as I predicted, the Mystics didn't make the playoffs.

I would never again coach in the WNBA, which saddens me to this day. But I wasn't ready to retire from the game of basketball—not hardly. I already had other irons in the fire.

16

A Basketball-Shaped World

I never thought that basketball would take me, this Jersey kid, all over the world. I was just hoping it would take me from high school to a college job, and to a nice little career. But this long strange trip took me from high school, to college, to the NBA, to high school again, to the NBA again, to the WNBA, and then to places all over the world I never dreamed of going to, much less coach at.

Because of recruiting overseas players into the WNBA, I often found myself in Russia and Eastern Europe, where some of the best female talent was coming from. Just as in any other profession, if you're in pro basketball long enough you make contacts and build relationships. I first went to Russia in 1999 and started coaching there in 2003, after I met a Lithuanian-born Russian oligarch named Shabtai von Kalmanovich, who, for as long as I knew him, simply went by the one-word moniker—Shabtai.

From the first day I met Shabtai he was a mystery wrapped in an enigma. Little by little, I began learning about his past, but his story always had several variations. He evidently was born in 1947 to poor Jewish parents, and his mother was a Holocaust survivor. He supposedly moved to Israel in 1971 and became the campaign manager to Prime Minister Golda Meir and also an Israeli spy. Later, though, he spent six years in an Israeli prison for being a Russian KGB spy. Or was it

five years? Rumor and innuendo had it that former U.S. secretary of state Henry Kissinger engineered his release. When
I met Shabtai, the sketchy details were that he was spying for
the Russian KGB. Then I heard he was a double agent. I even
heard he was a triple agent. It was all very hard to keep track of.

And then there were all the swirling stories about how
Shabtai amassed his staggering fortune, with reports saying
he was a billionaire. One story had it that he smuggled blood
diamonds from Sierra Leone. Another said he was in the con-
struction business. Yet another narrative was that he got wealthy
from shopping centers. Was it any of those? Or maybe all of
the above? Nobody seemed to know for sure, least of all me.
One thing was certain—Shabtai was politically connected,
as well as connected with some of Russia's most notorious
crime figures. Come to think of it, it was probably one in the
same. I even heard that Shabtai was in Vladimir Putin's cabi-
net. But, then again, as with everything about Shabtai, I didn't
know for sure.

Shabtai had expensive passions. He became a world-
renowned collector of Jewish art and religious objects—
specifically an enormous collection of eighteenth- and
nineteenth-century Torah scrolls, mezuzahs, menorahs, and
archival documents, which he displayed in a sort of mini-
museum. Because of his love for music and performers, he
promoted concerts, organizing extravagant shows for the likes
of Michael Jackson, Liza Minnelli, José Carreras, and Tom Jones.
He was rumored to have been romantically involved with Liza
Minnelli, and he once hired Tom Jones to perform at one of his
birthday parties. Luciano Pavarotti was one of his close friends,
as was a famous Russian crooner named Iosif Kobzon, who
was called the Soviet Sinatra and specialized in Yiddish songs.

Through all of this, the one passion that connected me to
Shabtai was his love of basketball. He owned a women's team in
Russia and was a major sponsor for Israel's top women's team.
His adopted hometown was Ekaterinburg, which was Russia's
fourth-largest city and about one thousand miles east of Mos-

cow, in notorious Siberia. Shabtai's team played for a while in Ekaterinburg, as well as in Moscow. Shortly after I met him, he asked me to become the team's consultant. Apparently, as I soon learned, in Russian lingo a consultant is another name for the head coach. It paid well. Very well. I took the job.

I enjoyed Shabtai. Most people did. It was hard not to love the guy, to be enamored by him. He was exceedingly charming, cheerful, a good listener, and above all he was generous. When you talked with Shabtai, he had the ability to make you believe you were the most important person in the world to him. It was not uncommon for him to pay foreign players, especially Americans, up to ten times more money than they were making in the WNBA. He would also provide them with luxurious housing—some of the top players were living in mansions.

As I got to know Shabtai better and better, I felt more and more comfortable probing him for background information. One day, I blurted out, "How many people have you killed, Shabtai?" I was joking. But he wasn't joking with his answer, and it chilled me. He wouldn't answer me directly. But he did tell me that sometimes making people suffer was better than killing them.

When Shabtai asked me to coach the club team Spartak Moscow in the inaugural World Cup for women's basketball, I paused for a variety of reasons. First of all, it didn't seem right for a guy like me, who bleeds red, white, and blue, to coach a team representing another country—especially a *Russian* team. At the time, the USA World Cup team was to be coached by former NBA star Michael Cooper, who was then coaching the Los Angeles Sparks. We had just lost to Cooper's Sparks in the WNBA Finals, so I thought he would offer me the assistant's job on the World Cup team. But I never heard from Cooper, or, for that matter, anybody from the USA contingent. So I figured, why not coach a Russian team? It was also an opportunity to coach on the world stage, and the challenge intrigued me.

The second thing that made me pause was my awareness that I was putting myself in dangerous situations. Shabtai knew I could win games for him. At the same time, I knew there were times when he was paying off officials whenever he thought it was necessary. That was Shabtai. And Russia, too. Corrupt to the core. It rattled me. Armed guards always accompanied Shabtai's teams. There were times when we stayed in hotels that he owned, where it seemed as if we were in an armed military camp with guards everywhere, even on the roof. For a Jersey guy who spent a lot of time in New York City, I thought I'd seen it all and was wise to the ways of the world. But this was a different world than anything I had ever experienced.

Shabtai wasn't much to look at. He had a boxer's nose, droopy eyes, and thin, perpetually pursed lips. But he dressed impeccably, usually in expensive European suits, and combed his thick, wavy black hair back and wore it flowing down past his collar. More than anything, the guy had a magnetic charisma about him. And, like me, he loved basketball. He built a beautiful, ten-thousand-seat arena in Ekaterinburg, modeling it after the Miami Heat's original arena, even replicating its orange seats. His teams always flew on his private plane, too. Needless to say, it didn't take much for him to convince me to coach a Russian team.

We had a good team and we were winning, and I'd like to think that we were winning legitimately. Early on, we even beat Michael Cooper's very good USA team. Eventually, we progressed to the Final Four for the World Cup Championship, which meant a lot to me. I liked our chances. I had practiced and drilled the team, and I knew they were prepared. I had two Russian assistant coaches and we got along real well. It was a fun team with talented players, and now we were matched up in the semifinals of the World Cup against Samara, a city about 650 miles southeast of Moscow, which Russia's other club team called home.

Just before the game, Shabtai came into my office and said, "Coach, coach, we have great wins. We are in semifinals. But we do not win tonight. We lose game tonight."

I thought I was hearing things. Looking at him as if he had two heads, I said, "Shabtai, we're playing for the World Cup Championship. That's what we worked hard for—to get here and win. This is what it's all about. This is the World Cup. The *World Cup!*"

"No, no. We would rather lose tonight," he said. "We give them game tonight and then later they will give us Russian League Championship. We would rather be Russian League champions than World Cup champions. World Cup is nice, but more prestige being Russia champion."

"Shabtai, no! I can't do that!"

"I give you more money," he said. With that, he pulled an envelope from his jacket and showed me how it was full with U.S. dollars. "There is $20,000 in here. It is for you."

"It's not a question of money," I said. "I've never thrown a game, and I never will."

Then he reached into the other side of his jacket and pulled out another envelope and said, "Here is another $20,000. Take it."

"Shabtai, I don't throw games. But if this is what you want to do, I'll let the two assistants take over and coach the team."

I joke now that if he had pulled out another envelope I might have changed my mind, but the truth is, I would never do that. I would never throw a game. I don't care what someone offered me. I ended up sitting behind the bench while the assistants coached the game. Going into the fourth quarter, the team was winning by 12 points. That's when the assistants followed the script and pulled out our best player, Elena Baranova, and two other starters. We lost. I was miserable. But Shabtai was ecstatic.

It was during this time that basketball began taking me around the world—both through coaching teams and doing clinics. Women's basketball and the World Cup took me to Argentina and Brazil. I did men's basketball clinics in China and Japan. Opportunities to do various clinics in France, Spain, and Belgium also came my way. The wNBA had me traveling to Poland, Lithuania, and the Czech Republic to recruit players. Italy was one of my favorite places to go, and I once did a clinic there in the city of Forlì with Hubie Brown, Doug Moe, Dr. Jack Ramsay, and Bill Walton. A few times, from 1989 to 1991, I did clinics in Italy for the National Basketball Coaches Association, run by my dear friend Michael Goldberg. That meant we could bring our wives and have their expenses paid. Carol and I went once with Orlando Woolridge and his wife, another time with Alvin Robertson and his wife, and one time I went alone with Joe Dumars and his wife. Alex, Joe, and Orlando were all great guys, as well as great former NBA stars.

Traveling and coaching in clinics with some of the all-time great basketball minds was a highlight for me. I learned a lot, and in those relaxed settings, where you're not just coaching but also socializing with the guys, you get to really know personalities. It was always a lot of fun. One of the most impressive guys I met was Dr. Jack Ramsay, and not just because of his basketball genius. He was also a physical specimen. One time, after doing a clinic, several of us were hanging out at the beach on the Adriatic Sea. Without a word, Dr. Ramsay got up, walked to the water, waded in, and started swimming out. It wasn't long before the only thing you could see was his bald head glistening in the sun, getting farther and farther away from us. And then—gone. No bald head. Nothing.

"Should we worry?" I asked, although the pronoun *we* wasn't exactly accurate, because *I* was already worried.

"Nah," said Bill Walton. "He's in great shape. The guy does triathlons."

I tried to relax, often staring at the beach with dogged intensity. What seemed like an hour later, I saw a bald head bobbing in the surf, moving toward us. Soon enough, Dr. Jack Ramsay was back on the beach, drying himself off as if nothing happened, as if he'd just enjoyed a leisurely walk in the park. That was Dr. Ramsay. Until the day he died, at age eighty-nine, he was always in tip-top shape for his age.

Carol and I would usually time those coaching trips to Italy so that we could spend extra time there and vacation. After a clinic one year in Sicily, we decided to take a vacation and head to the Amalfi Coast. My cousin, Mike Adubato, who had been in the military supporting NATO, had spent a few years in Naples. He warned me about traveling in Italy.

"They'll try to trick you," he said. "They'll drive close behind your car and start beeping the horn, pretending something is wrong with your car, to get you to pull over. Don't do it! Once you pull over, they're gonna rob you. Plus, they've been known to leave a few dead bodies along the roadside."

After the clinic, Carol and I flew to Naples and rented a car from Avis. When we signed the paperwork the manager showed us our car, which was not the one we thought we had rented. But he told us it was a nicer car, which it was. We loaded our luggage, jumped in, and headed out. As we drove away, all I could think of was what my cousin Mike had said. With my eyes scanning the rearview mirror, I missed the exit for the highway we were supposed to take going south. I made a U-turn and doubled back. Just then I looked in the rearview mirror and saw a car right behind us with two old guys in it. They were beeping their horn, getting my attention, and pointing at my tire.

"Didn't your cousin Mike tell you that this is the trick they use?" Carol asked.

"Yeah, but these are old guys, and it's still daylight, and we're on a busy road. What can happen?"

"Old guys?" Carol said. "Have you looked in a mirror lately?"

Thinking it was safe, I pulled over, and they pulled in behind us. One guy stayed in the car while the other guy got out, walked up to us, and pointed to the right rear tire. That's when I noticed that the hubcap was off. I thought maybe the lug nuts might be loose so I went into the trunk to get the lug wrench. Carol got out and was holding her pocketbook, and the guy said it was probably safer to leave it in the car because somebody might come by and snatch it from her.

Just then, another car rolled in front of us and boxed us in. A guy got out, and I could see he was going for the driver's side of our rental car. I might be stupid, but not that stupid.

I turned and whacked the one guy hard with the lug wrench right across his thigh, and he went down hard. I went after the guy trying to get into my rental car, and he ran. I took a swipe before he got back in his car and clipped him across his right shoulder. Both cars were soon speeding away. Our car, too. But not without Carol cursing me the whole trip, reminding me again and again what my cousin Mike had told me, and what an idiot I was. She was right, of course. It gave me chills when I finally found the road going south that I had missed, and couldn't help but notice that it was a quiet, lonely road, with few cars; much different than the busy road we had just left. Had I pulled over on that road, things might have been different—much different.

International travel can be dangerous that way. But nothing offered the element of danger that being around Shabtai presented. I was always thankful that when I was in Russia, my agent, Bruce Levy, was usually with me. Bruce had a way of calming me and also a way of communicating with Shabtai, because they had one important thing in common—they were both Jewish. Although Shabtai was Russian, he considered himself Jewish first. So naturally he had basketball ties in Israel. After he got to know me, and liked me, Shabtai talked to me about coaching the team he sponsored in Israel. I had never been to Israel, but Bruce had, and he told me we would go together. It helped, too, that Shabtai's team had two players that I had coached with the Liberty—Crystal Robinson and Vickie Johnson.

When Bruce and I flew on El Al Israel Airlines from New York City to Tel Aviv, I had never seen such great security. They didn't just question you before you boarded. They *interrogated* you. I'll say this, though—I never felt safer getting on a flight.

When we arrived in Israel, Shabtai had us booked at the Hilton Tel Aviv Hotel, which was one of the most beautiful hotels I've ever stayed at. My room was on the tenth floor and it was just gorgeous, with a stunning view overlooking the Mediterranean Sea. It's where most businessmen and politicians and international dignitaries stay when they are in Israel. But instead of all the security making me feel secure, it spooked me. I had an overwhelming feeling that something was going to happen, and if it was going to happen, the target would be where important people were.

Sure enough, the hotel alarms went off in the middle of the first night, blaring with an ominous wail. I bolted out of bed and could see lights flashing from below. The alarms were actually coming from outside, and as I looked out the window I saw Israeli soldiers everywhere, brandishing automatic weapons. A bunch swarmed around three taxicabs. People had their hands up. Some were pinned against trees.

The next morning I called Shabtai. "I don't want to stay here at the Hilton," I said. "Do me a favor and book me somewhere else."

"Richie, you must stay there. It is most beautiful hotel. The food is great. Everything centrally located."

I told him what happened the night before.

"Yes, but nothing did happen because security is so good."

"Maybe that's true," I said. "But please find me a Motel 6 or something like that—just a little motel about two stories high that nobody knows about, nobody cares about, and that I can run out of quickly."

Shabtai tried to wear me down. My agent tried to wear me down. It didn't work. I moved anyway. My nerves were shot staying at the Hilton. I couldn't take it anymore.

There were six teams in the league and it was a different way of coaching because the games were played on Friday nights. Teams practiced Monday through Thursday and then ended the week with a Friday night game. Coaching that way, playing only once a week, made it hard to keep focus. But you adjust.

Our general manager owned a restaurant in Tel Aviv and we would go there after games. One night, toward the end of the season, I walked in and saw a handful of chairs at the front of the restaurant with a head table attached to them. I asked what the chairs were for. Our GM told me that since the season was ending and the playoffs were about to start, they would like for me to say a few words. "Sure, no problem," I said. "But I'm gonna tell you right now to take those chairs and the head table and move them to the back of the restaurant, and I'll be happy to speak." I kept being told it was safe, but I wasn't buying it. "Listen, I didn't grow up in New Jersey for nothin'," I said. "You never have a meeting in front of glass. Put it in the back of the restaurant and I'll have no problem." They finally capitulated, and it turned out to be a great evening.

Two weeks later, the restaurant directly across the street was blown up. A Palestinian woman exploded herself, the explosives evidently concealed in her orifices. Shards and debris reached across the street. You can have all the security you want, but if someone wants to blow themselves up, it's tough to stop that.

With the help of my two star players from the Liberty—Crystal Robinson and Vickie Johnson—we won the playoffs. It was a great season, a great playoff series, and an overall great experience. My only regret is that I never got to Jerusalem. I was going to take Crystal and Vickie and go, but when I called them up, they said they didn't want to go on that day.

"Why not?"

"It's a Muslim holiday," they said. "There could be a million Muslims in Jerusalem that day."

I was going to go without them, but I decided against it. A few days later, when I left Israel to go back to the States, there were a couple of older women who were returning from a tour of Israel. Not only was Jerusalem part of the tour, they had gone on the day I didn't go. They talked about how much they loved it, and how great it was. I thought: These were women, older than me, and they weren't afraid to go to Jerusalem that day. What a chicken I was.

Although I loved Shabtai, I never felt totally comfortable with him, or around him. There was always this sense that something could happen at any moment—something not good. He had a temper, and he wasn't a guy to be pissed off or double-crossed. I had not forgotten, nor I'm sure had he, that I had defied him by not being complicit and throwing that game. Adding to my unease was my awareness of how easily things could get tangled trying to communicate across languages and cultures.

Even still, I didn't think twice when one year I brought Elena Baranova back with me from Russia, so that she and her six-foot-five frame could play for me on the New York Liberty. It wasn't as if I was taking her away from playing on Shabtai's Russian national team because the seasons were different—the WNBA played in the summer and in Russia they played in the winter.

Well, when Shabtai heard that Baranova was with me, he called my agent. "Richie steal Baranova," he told Bruce. "I kill him."

I took it seriously. Just because I was in New York City didn't mean I was safe, especially since there were now hundreds of thousands of Russians with a growing mafia presence living in Brooklyn's Brighton Beach area, only a short subway ride from Madison Square Garden. Shabtai was connected, and his connections could easily reach to where I was. I recalled how he said sometimes it was better to make people suffer rather than kill them. I wasn't sleeping well. I finally asked Bruce to give me Shabtai's phone number, and I called him.

"Shabtai," I said, "please listen to me. I know you're upset about me taking Baranova, but she wanted to come. She wanted to play in the WNBA. I didn't think you'd care because we play opposite seasons. We're May, June, July, and August. You're October through April. She'll be a much better player because of the experience here. We'll work with her for four months. Our league has much better competition than the Russian league. So you'll be happy with the results."

The more I talked to him, the more I think he got it.

"Okay," he finally said. "I'm glad you call because I was not looking at total picture. I feel better now."

I sighed, probably audibly, because I felt better too. Still, I wasn't sure. A few days later I called Bruce and asked if everything was really okay with Shabtai. He assured me it was. Still, it was always that kind of high-wire act with Shabtai. He would often tell me that he wanted to buy an NBA team—and he had the money to do it—and make me the head coach, which I loved hearing. But because of his Russian espionage background, I knew that was never going to happen. Shabtai couldn't get into the United States, much less have access to buying an NBA team—though years later another billionaire Russian oligarch, Mikhail Prokhorov, bought the Brooklyn Nets. Point is, it was always that way with Shabtai—one moment he could be talking about buying an NBA team and the next talking about killing you.

My last year coaching in Russia was 2006. The winters were brutal, and I just couldn't take the cold anymore. I got tired of hearing the words *twenty below* day after day after day. Bruce was with me and our last flight out was scheduled to take us from Ekaterinburg to Moscow. From there we were to fly to Prague and then to New York.

As we walked across the tarmac in Ekaterinburg, I noticed that it wasn't twenty below—it was twenty-three below! Snow was falling, ice was everywhere, and we could hardly walk without slipping. Through the snow I could make out the faint outline of the Ural Mountains; mountains that I knew we had to fly over. To make matters worse, it was a prop plane. How in the world are we going to climb over those mountains with this plane and in these conditions? Convinced that I was going to die, and likely end up in hell, I turned to my agent and said, "Bruce, I know that in the Jewish religion you don't have hell. I've heard that. As a Catholic, we have heaven, we have purgatory, and we have hell. So if you have any Jewish prayers that can convert me, I want to be converted right now."

He laughed, and we got on the plane. As we boarded, I noticed ice on the wings. I also noticed that they weren't de-icing the plane. I was scared to death. Speaking in broken English, the two pilots tried to assure me that it was "no problem" and that they "do it all the time."

After we took off, I opened my eyes long enough to see through the falling snow that we were safely clearing the Ural Mountains. We got into Moscow at 3 a.m., caught our next flight four hours later, went through Prague, and eventually back to New York. That was the end of my Russian experience.

Years later, on November 2, 2009, I was sitting in my home-office in Orlando when my daughter Beth called me from Los Angeles. "Dad," she asked, "wasn't the guy you worked for in Russia named Shabtai von Kalmanovich?"

"Yeah," I said. "Why?"

"He's not around anymore," Beth said. "They shot up his car in Moscow and killed him."

"Oh my god!" I exclaimed. I was glad I was sitting down. My mind raced to what, why, when, who?

I checked the news, hoping it was a mistake, but my daughter was correct. Shabtai had been assassinated, and it was a professional hit, for sure. The gunmen waited until his chauffeur-driven Mercedes s500 was at a traffic light several hundred yards from Putin's central office, when they unloaded a hail of gunfire into it. I knew that Mercedes s500 well because I had ridden in it many times. Reports said Shabtai was hit eighteen times, and at sixty-one years old, he was killed instantly. Reports also said investigators found $1.5 million in U.S. dollars in his car.

All these years later, his murder remains unsolved.

17

The Sound and the Funny

A s hard as coaching is, I miss it all the time. For some reason, though, there comes a point where *old coaches* are viewed as just *old*, and we move on to other aspects of the game that do not require us to have a whistle dangling from our necks.

When I was coaching in the WNBA and overseas, it wasn't my only job. I also got into broadcasting, and right from the start I enjoyed the heck out of it. The beauty of broadcasting is that all the years you spent coaching, and the insights and connections you have, now work to your favor. Your age now becomes a plus. It's a paradox. You're too old, or so they say, to sit courtside with a team, but because you're so old, or so they think, you now have a head full of knowledge that you can spew into a microphone. Later in my career, when I reached that age where I was viewed more as *old* instead of as an *old coach*, I reconnected with the Orlando Magic and became a color commentator—with the emphasis on the *color* part. That's just me. When I coached the Magic, I was known for my colorful suits, shirts, and ties. The *Orlando Sentinel* once did a feature on me, focusing mostly on my colorful attire. They even took a photo of me in my closet. That colorful persona is my personality, and I brought that to the broadcast booth.

I soon learned, however, that being colorful and being politically correct doesn't always go hand in hand.

In one of my early broadcasts I used a term that I didn't think twice about. It's a term used when someone is a little wobbly, especially if they've been hit in the head. I grew up hearing it described as "Queer Street." So one night, while I was broadcasting a game, one of the Magic players got hit hard in the head and was dazed. "It looks like he's on Queer Street," I said. Needless to say, everybody jumped all over me for that. I kept telling anyone who would listen what my intent was, but nobody seemed to get it. So I googled it and showed everyone how it's a term used when someone gets clocked in the head and gets up a bit woozy. I was informed that it was still best not to use the term.

Another time, when the Magic were getting outrebounded, I barked into the microphone, "Our guys are rebounding like a bunch of midgets!" My play-by-play radio partner, Dennis Neumann, corrected me. "You can't say 'midgets' or 'dwarfs' anymore," he said. "It's politically incorrect. You have to use the term 'little people.'" Somehow, saying "little people" lost something in translation. So I refused to use it.

I'm not afraid to sing on the radio, either. It must be the Italian in me. If the Magic are getting blown out, I'll croon, "Mama said there'd be days like this . . ." Or if the Magic win, I might belt, "Celebrate good times—come on!" and, "We will, we will rock you!" After a Magic player blocks a shot I'll launch into, "He did the Mash! He did the Monster Mash! It was a foul line smash!"

I do take pronouncing names seriously, though. Because of all the time spent overseas, I learned how to pronounce some real tongue twisters. It came in handy with NBA players, since so many of them come from foreign countries.

When the Magic traded Dwight Howard and one of the players they got in return was a young center named Nikola Vučević, I immediately knew from my travels to Eastern Europe that his name was not pronounced *Vuk-ah-vick*, as if the *c* had a *k* sound. Instead, when you see a *c* in a name like that, it's pronounced with a *ch*, so that you say *Vootch-ah-vitch*. A lot of folks were mispronouncing Vučević's name early in his career—but not me.

One night, I was broadcasting a game with the Magic playing the Minnesota Timberwolves, who had a center named Nikola Petrović. During the pregame broadcast, I noted that Vučević and Petrović were both strong, physical centers, and I made the comment that it was going to be a battle beneath the boards. "Let's see who wins the battle of the vitches," I said. I thought it was funny, but our producer wasted no time telling me to cut it out. I turned to him and said, "Well, I guess I can't say they're both sons of vitches." He looked at me, smiled, and said, "Not if you want two months off." For weeks, though, I kept running into fans on the street when I was out and about, telling me they loved it when I said "battle of the vitches" and that I should use it again. They thought it was hilarious. But they also weren't the ones paying my salary.

Sometimes, however, pronouncing names correctly is difficult for a Jersey guy like me. I can sympathize because people have butchered the pronunciation of my name all my life. It's Ah-due-bah-toe. Once you get the hang of it, it's fairly simple. I've been called Allababa, Abracadabra, Addaboodo, and a host of other names—some of which have nothing to do with my last name. For two years with the Orlando Magic, Shaquille O'Neal called me AduBAYdo. I finally corrected him one day and told him if he kept calling me AduBAYdo that I was going to call him Shiq. He started pronouncing my name correctly—except nowadays he's back to saying AduBAYdo whenever he sees me, doing so with that sly lopsided smile of his. One year, when Ricky Pitino and I were assistants for Hubie Brown on the New York Knicks, I was living in West Orange, New Jersey, and Pitino was living in Livingston, New Jersey. Pitino had been to my house, and the next day he was trying to reach me but had lost my phone number. He called information and asked for a Richie Adubato on 15 Harvard Terrace in West Orange, which was my address. After a long pause as the operator attempted to find the number, she told him, "I'm sorry but I'm not finding that name at that address." Pitino insisted that she was wrong and he was not taking no for an answer. "I was there yesterday," he said. "I know he's there and he has a phone. It's Richie Adubato at 15 Harvard Terrace in West Orange." The operator went right back at Pitino, saying, "And I'm telling you there is no Richie's Auto Body at that address in West Orange."

The names I struggle with are those from Asia. That became evident when the Magic were in China playing the Chinese national team. I just couldn't get the names of some of those players to come off my tongue the right way. About the only name I could pronounce correctly was that of a small forward named Wong Fong Yu. So if somebody scored a bucket and I couldn't pronounce the name, I'd lean into the microphone and say, "Basket by Wong Fong Yu." Or, "A three-pointer by Wong Fong Yu."

The next day, Scott Anez, one of the radio guys I work with, jokingly said to me, "Hey Richie, I was looking at the box score and this guy Wong Fong Yu, I thought he'd have like 35 points. Turns out he only had 10." We both got a good laugh out of that.

As you would expect from an old coach, I am always on the officials. Here are some of the things I say if one of our guys is fouled hard but the officials didn't call it:

"No autopsy, no foul."

"He'd be safer on a New York City subway."

And if the official just flat missed the call, here are some of my favorites:

"He can't help it. His father was a lookout on the *Titanic*."

"He missed that call. I guess he was too close, because maybe he's farsighted."

"Maybe his glass eye fogged up."

"We've got three officials tonight—two good ones and Mr. Magoo."

"Stevie Wonder could've made that call! And they still missed it!"

Once, on a road trip in Los Angeles, the broadcasting crew was eating at a Cheesecake Factory in Marina del Rey. As I gazed across the restaurant, I spotted Stevie Wonder sitting in the corner with a woman who appeared to be his bodyguard. Since he's one of my all-time favorites, I knew I had to talk to him. I also seemed to recall that he was a basketball fan. As I walked over, the woman stood up to meet me before I got to Stevie. "Excuse me, I'm Richie Adubato. I'm an ex-NBA head coach now doing radio with the Orlando Magic. I used to be with the Knicks, and I'd love to talk to Stevie." I was thrilled when he invited me to sit with him and have a cup of coffee.

"I remember when you were with the Knicks," Stevie said. "Back when they had Bill Cartwright, Bernard King, and all those guys!" Right away, I was impressed by his basketball knowledge. Our chat went like that for a while—talking sports with Stevie Wonder—just a real pleasant conversation. When I got up to leave, I thanked him for his time and said, "I knew it. I knew you were a fan."

When I got back to my table with the broadcasting team, Dennis Neumann smiled and asked me if I told Stevie that I'm fond of saying on air, "Stevie Wonder could've made that call!"

Uh, no.

The most difficult thing to do as a broadcaster, especially if you are an old coach like me, is to criticize a head coach. Only coaches know how hard coaching is, especially if you don't have the players. I sometimes think of Pat Riley who had four NBA titles under his belt before the 2002–3 NBA season when he was Miami's head coach. But that season, the Heat went 25-57. Why? Because they didn't have the players. The Heat's three double-digit scorers that season were Eddie Jones, Caron Butler, and Brian Grant. Three seasons later, when the Heat had Shaquille O'Neal and Dwyane Wade, Riley won his fifth NBA title. Riley's last season as a head coach was 2007–8, and the Heat went 15-67. It happens. If you don't have the players, you're not going to get too many of those Ws.

I also sometimes think of Larry Brown, who is the only coach in history to have won an NCAA National Championship (Kansas Jayhawks in 1988) and an NBA Championship (Detroit Pistons in 2004). Yet, two years after winning that NBA title, one of the greatest Xs and Os tacticians in basketball history coached the New York Knicks to a 23-59 record. Brown also coached the 1988–89 San Antonio Spurs team to a 21-61 record. The difference? Players. It always and invariably comes down to players.

So I am loath to criticize a coach. If you look at a list of Hall of Fame coaches, about the only one you will find who did not have a losing record—or two, or three, or four—is Phil Jackson. Why? Because Phil Jackson coached teams with Michael Jordan, Scottie Pippen, Kobe Bryant, and Shaquille O'Neal on them—that's why. That isn't to say that Phil Jackson isn't a great coach. Of course he is. He just never had to try to win when his three best players were Eddie Jones, Caron Butler, and Brian Grant.

18

Havin' a Ball

The start of the 2020–21 NBA season found me entering my sixtieth year in basketball—involved in the game I love and living the life I love. There might be somebody else who has been a head coach at the high school level, the college level, in the NBA, in the WNBA, and internationally—but I can't come up with another name. And then you have to add to that a career behind the microphone broadcasting basketball. It's been quite a ride, and I've enjoyed every step of the way. When you feel as blessed as I do, you can't help but sometimes think about how it all might have gone differently. I also sometimes think of how many times my life could have ended prematurely.

There were foolish things I did, crazy risks I took, like the time when I was a young man and I chased those Cuban thugs into an empty parking lot in the Meadowlands of New Jersey and went after them with my big DeSoto, busting the open doors off their car only to have them shoot at me. The next day there were bullet holes in my DeSoto, but thankfully not in me. That's how close it was. But when you're young, you think you're invincible.

The older you get, you don't take close calls for granted. And for some reason I've had my share of close calls.

I almost got shot at again, years later in 1999, when I

was with a car dealer friend of mine named Jerry Jones at a basketball tournament at Disney's Wide World of Sports Complex in Orlando. After the game we went to a local Ale House restaurant that I frequent. Jerry and I were sitting there, eating and chatting, when gunfire ripped through the normal bustling noise of a sports bar restaurant. Jerry and I ducked under the table we were sitting at and tried to determine what was happening. It sounded like the shots were coming from another room, maybe the office or the kitchen. Unbeknownst to me, Jerry had a concealed weapon permit and he was carrying a small handgun with a couple of bullets in it.

"Don't worry," he said. "I'm a deadly shot. If anybody comes this way, I'll get 'em."

"Look, I don't like our position here," I said. "We're in the middle of the bar, in the middle of everything. We could easily get shot. Stay low and follow me. We're breaking past the pool tables and diving out through the front door. C'mon! Let's get outta here!"

We made it to the door and dived onto the ground outside, thinking we were safe. Instead of being some type of horrific mass shooting, it was two guys committing a robbery. Just after we tumbled out the door, lying on the ground, one of the robbers ran out, almost stepping over us as he fled. Thank goodness he never broke stride, and as he kept running for his getaway car, we ran back inside the restaurant, where we saw the other robber on the floor bleeding badly from a gunshot wound, courtesy of an off-duty Orlando police officer who worked security for the restaurant. Before we knew it, the cops surrounded the place. Eventually they caught the other guy. It was breaking news on the local TV stations, and one of our friends who knew I liked to hang out at the Ale House called my wife, Carol. "Did you see the news about the shooting at the Ale House?" she asked. "I didn't see it," Carol replied, "but I just got off the phone with Richie. He called and told me he was right in the middle of it." That was me—

always seemingly in the middle of something and always seemingly coming away unscathed.

When I was coaching the Dallas Mavericks, we had a season ticket holder named Vernon Peppard who was an oil millionaire and a pilot who owned his own plane. Vernon was always happy to fly me around, which was great because it saved me a lot of time. His plane was a six-seater, and usually there would be a pilot, a copilot, Vernon, and I. We would sit back, relax, and travel in no time back and forth to where I needed to be.

One time, I had to go to Little Rock, Arkansas, and when I got to the airport to fly with Vernon it was just him and me.

"Where are the pilot and copilot?" I said.

"The pilot had a chance to go work for American Airlines," Vernon said. "And the copilot is sick. But I can fly the plane. No problem."

We climbed onboard and I got in the back. After we got airborne, I was reading the newspaper and drinking a cup of coffee, when I suddenly recalled that Vernon, who was sixty-five at the time, had a bad heart. He'd had some heart attacks and surgeries. Like a slap in the face, the thought hit me: *We have no copilot. It's just me and Vernon, who has a bad heart.* By then it was too late to back out. As we flew toward Little Rock, a dark rain cloud emerged on the horizon like an ominous omen. Soon, it started raining hard, with violent pellets of water smacking the plane as it shook. I was shaking even more. Vernon muscled the plane over the top of the rain cloud, came around, and landed at the airport. I breathed a sigh of relief.

"I've got to fly right back," Vernon said as I gathered my stuff—both physically and emotionally. "But I'll come back tomorrow and bring you home."

"Hey, don't worry about it. Don't go out of your way," I said. "I'll get a car and drive back. I love to drive."

I hate to drive.

It was about a dozen years later when I heard that Vernon died of a heart attack—thankfully, it wasn't while piloting a plane.

The other part about getting older is that you find yourself losing too many of your friends, colleagues, and players. The sweet spot of my career as an NBA coach, unfortunately, was also when the league had a serious drug problem—mostly with cocaine. I often think of Roy Tarpley, and I'm haunted with the knowledge that despite all my efforts to try to save him from that dark tunnel of addiction, I couldn't. Such a talent. Such a sweet man. Such a shame. Dead at fifty.

Once, when I did a clinic in Italy with former NBA star Orlando Woolridge, I really got to know him and I really liked him. Orlando was a lovely man who was hilariously funny. He and I also coached in the WNBA, so we had a lot of stories to share. On those warm Italian summer evenings, walking the streets, I used to stop to buy the sweetest watermelon I have ever tasted. It was the perfect dessert. Just delicious. Orlando's wife, Patricia, and I would get watermelon while Orlando, who hadn't kept his battles with drugs a secret, roamed the streets for something else. He died of heart failure at fifty-two—way too young.

There are others who didn't live out their days for as long as they should have—guys with incredible talent and outsized personalities. One of those personalities was Darryl Dawkins, who was the first guy to go straight from high school to the NBA, leaving Orlando's Maynard Evans High School for the Philadelphia 76ers in 1975. Darryl Dawkins was Shaquille O'Neal way before Shaq. He was a beast beneath the boards who shattered rims with thunderous dunks and was a fun-loving guy off the court. Like Shaq, Darryl also had a nickname for everything and everyone—including himself. The one that stuck with him was Chocolate Thunder. When I was a New York Knicks assistant coach, I got to know the New Jersey Nets owner, Joe Taub, who was a Jersey guy like me—from Paterson. We were having dinner and drinks one night after the game with an executive from a sneaker company that represented Dawkins. The executive got a phone call he needed to take. Evidently, Dawkins was supposed to be at a promotional function for the sneaker company but had refused to show up unless there was $10,000 worth of cocaine waiting for him on a table. I'm fairly sure they got it to him. Dawkins died of a heart attack at fifty-eight.

Although I've been around drug addiction, I've never really understood its pull or the desire. I'll enjoy a cocktail or two, and that's as strong as it gets. But given how reckless I was in other ways when I was younger, I feel fortunate to have not only made it as far as I have but to still feel on top of my game, and have that game be working in basketball. Being in sports is a wonderful way to make a living, so I was happy to see my children also get involved with sports during their adult lives. Scott and Beth, from my first marriage, have turned out to be great adults, as has my son Adam, from my marriage with Carol. I'm proud of all three of them. Scott became a heck of a basketball player, earning a scholarship to Upsala College, and in 1987 he was drafted in the seventh round by the Sacramento Kings. He made it until the last cut during camp and is now a coach, and has coached all over the world. Beth made a career as a sports broadcaster in TV and radio, while also doing some acting on the side, and today she is a college professor with a doctorate degree. And Adam got his law degree from Florida State University, with an undergraduate degree in sports management. He is pursuing a career as a sports agent.

Time marches on, and it's time for another generation to make its mark. But my generation isn't through yet. The only one from our original Jersey Guys to have passed away is Rollie Massimino. Cancer took Rollie in 2017, at eighty-two. The rest of us are all still going strong, and still involved in basketball—almost all of us now in broadcasting. I continue to provide radio color commentary for Orlando Magic broadcasts. Hubie Brown is a TV analyst. Mike Fratello is also a TV analyst. Brian Hill, whom I coached in high school and coached with in the NBA, is part of the Magic broadcasting team. And then there is my best friend, Dick Vitale, who is as excitable as ever as college basketball's beloved broadcasting legend. Just listen to any of us and you won't just hear our passion for the game, you'll *feel* it.

It's funny that so many of us have gravitated to broadcasting, and yet we've never so much as mentioned it to each other. Then again, nothing needs to be mentioned. We know why we're in broadcasting. We've gone from old coaches to just being *old*, but it's acknowledged that we have the knowledge, and we can opine about today's game while also speaking about the greats and the great matchups from yesterday. So we get hired as analysts and color commentators. And while it's not coaching, it's the next best thing because it keeps us in the game and keeps us involved in something we are passionate about—talking basketball and being around coaches and players. Just listen to Dickie V, or any of us Jersey Guys on the air, and you won't just hear what we know about basketball, you'll also hear how much we love basketball. Though I am happy with broadcasting, at the same time, I still miss coaching. Heck, I still miss playing. But life goes on.

One thing I don't agree with is the notion that because you have gotten older it means you can't coach anymore, that you're somehow over the hill. But isn't that the way it usually works? I'm sure when we were young bucks, we got hired over some of the older coaches because it was perceived that we were youthful, energetic, had fresh ideas, and perhaps we could relate to players better. Maybe that's true. But as I mentioned, nothing replaces experience and the historical knowledge of the game. When I am watching an NBA player today, I can say that he reminds me of a Bob Lanier, or a Bob McAdoo, or a Kareem Abdul-Jabbar, or a Julius "Dr. J" Erving. I can say that because I saw all those great players with my own eyes. I coached some of them and coached against the others.

The other wonderful thing about basketball is that it has taken me all over the globe. North America, South America, Central America, Europe, Asia . . . into some great countries and cultures, meeting wonderful people. I didn't always speak the native language, but I could speak the universal language of basketball.

It's been quite a ride, an amazing journey, and I see no end in sight. Through it all, through all the twists and turns that life took me on, one thing has been constant: I've been havin' a ball.

APPENDIX

Coaching Timeline

Junior Varsity High School Coaching

1960–62: Stevens Academy, New Jersey (29-5)

1962–63: Saint Joseph's West, New York (15-2)

North Hudson County JV Champions

1963–65: Our Lady of the Valley, New Jersey (28-3)

Won 1964 Essex County JV Championship

Varsity High School Coaching

1965–69: Our Lady of the Valley, New Jersey (76-14)

1965 North Jersey State Champions Parochial B

Catholic Federation Champions in 1966 and 1967

College Coaching

1969–72: Upsala (NJ) College Freshman Team (42-8)

Victories over Division I programs: Seton Hall, St. Peters, Lafayette, and Fordham

1972–78: Upsala (NJ) College Varsity Team (100-53)

Won ECAC Division III Title in 1976

Went 19-9 in 1978 and earned school's first NCAA bid in twenty years

Key Notes and Accomplishments from High School and College Coaching

Record from 1960 to 1978: 290-85 (77.3 winning percentage)

New Jersey coaching contemporaries throughout these years included: Dick Vitale, Hubie Brown, Rollie Massimino, and Mike Fratello

Detroit Pistons Coaching

1978–79: Assistant Coach with Pistons under Dick Vitale

Team's star players included Bob Lanier and M. L. Carr

1979–80: Interim Head Coach with Pistons

Dick Vitale was fired after twelve games

Pistons traded Bob Lanier to Bucks after thirty-seven games

Bob McAdoo was injured for portion of season

Pistons had eleven players twenty-five years old or younger

New York Knicks Coaching

1982–86: Assistant Coach with Knicks under Hubie Brown

Advanced to back-to-back Eastern Conference Semi-finals (1983, 1984)

Pushed Boston Celtics (eventual champions) to seven games in 1984 playoffs

Team's star players included: Bernard King, Bill Cartwright, and Patrick Ewing

Notable assistant coaches: Mike Fratello, Rick Pitino, and Bob Hill

Dallas Mavericks Coaching

1986–87: Assistant Coach with Mavericks under Dick Motta

Team finished 55-27 and qualified for playoffs

Motta retired after season

1987–88: Assistant Coach with Mavericks under John MacLeod

Team finished 53-29 and advanced to Western Conference Finals

Defeated Rockets and Nuggets in first two rounds of playoffs and pushed Lakers (eventual champions) to seven games in conference finals

Team's star players included: Mark Aguirre, Derek Harper, Rolando Blackman, Sam Perkins, and Roy Tarpley

1988–89: Assistant Coach with Mavericks under John MacLeod

Roy Tarpley was suspended (played only nineteen games), and team was plagued with injuries

Mavs traded Mark Aguirre midseason for Adrian Dantley

1989–90: Head Coach with Mavericks

John MacLeod was fired after eleven games

Coached team to 42-29 record (59 winning percentage); was named permanent coach on April 22, 1990

Mavs went 19-3 at home with only losses at Reunion Arena to Lakers, Bulls, and Timberwolves

Mavs held a club-record thirty-five opponents to under 100 points (twelve of those opponents failed to reach 90 points)

Mavs ranked in top ten in most defensive categories (steals, blocks, and opponent field goal percentage)

Basketball America ranked Adubato the NBA's second-best coach

1. Chuck Daly, Pistons (59-32)

2. Richie Adubato, Mavs (42-29)

3. Del Harris, Bucks (44-38)

1990–91: Head Coach with Mavericks

Sam Perkins left Mavs to join Lakers in free agency prior to season

Started season 4-1 before Roy Tarpley suffered season-ending ACL injury (Tarpley averaged 24 points and 12.3 rebounds in four complete games)

Mavs still managed to rank in top ten in several defensive categories (opponent three-pointers made, steals, and fouls)

1991–92: Head Coach with Mavericks

Though team still had Rolando Blackman and Derek Harper, Mavs were one of youngest teams in league (nine players twenty-five years old or younger)

Roy Tarpley was suspended for entire season

1992–93: Head Coach with Mavericks

Fired after twenty-nine games

Derek Harper was only player on roster over thirty years old

Roy Tarpley was suspended for entire season

Rookie Jim Jackson only played in twenty-eight games all season

Cleveland Cavaliers Coaching

1993–94: Assistant Coach with Cavaliers under Mike Fratello

Despite tons of injuries (Brad Daugherty missed thirty-two games, Larry Nance missed forty-nine games), the Cavs won forty-seven games and made playoffs

Orlando Magic Coaching

1994–95: Assistant Coach with Magic under Brian Hill

Part of NBA All-Star Game coaching staff

Helped Magic reach NBA Finals for first time in franchise history

Magic ranked first in NBA in offensive rating

1995–96: Assistant Coach with Magic under Brian Hill

Helped Magic win franchise record sixty games

Swept Pistons and eliminated Hawks in five games

before getting swept by Michael Jordan's Bulls in conference finals

Magic ranked third in NBA in offensive rating

1996–97: Head Coach with Magic

Took over as head coach when Brian Hill was fired after forty-nine games

Went 21-12 as head coach to finish regular season and helped push Heat to decisive fifth game in first round of playoffs

Penny Hardaway had back-to-back 40-plus scoring performances in Games Three and Four against Heat

WNBA Coaching

1999–2004: Head Coach with New York Liberty

Advanced to WNBA Finals in three of the first four years and conference finals in four of five years with Liberty

Coached in three WNBA All-Star Games

2000 Pro Basketball Coach of the Year presented by New Jersey Sports Writers Association

Notable players coached: Becky Hammon, Vickie Johnson, Crystal Robinson, and Tari Phillips

2006: Head Coach with Washington Mystics

Advanced to first round of WNBA playoffs

Notable players coached: Alana Beard, DeLisha Milton-Jones, and Chasity Melvin

Left Mystics after four games of 2007 season

The only coach in history to lead two NBA teams and two WNBA teams to playoffs

Women's International Coaching

2003–4: Head Coach of UMMC Ekaterinburg (Russia)

Team won all nine Russian League games under Adubato's leadership

Finished in second place in FIBA World Cup (Samara, Russia)

Defeated Team USA in semifinals

Did not coach in championship game against Ukraine (team lost)

2004–5: Head Coach of Elitzur Ramla (Israel)

Team went 10-1 and won the Israeli League Championship

2005–6: Head Coach of Spartak Moscow Region (Russia)

Team went 14-2 and won the European Cup

Notable players coached: Lisa Leslie, Tamika Catchings, Crystal Robinson, Ticha Penicheiro, Natalie Williams, and Irina Osipova

Basketball Clinics and Camps

Did clinics for NBA under direction of Michael Goldberg (executive director of NBA Coaches Association) with stops in Italy, France, Spain, Mexico, Brazil, Argentina, Japan, and China

Taught drills with NBA players including Joe Dumars, Alvin Robertson, Orlando Woolridge, and Darrell Walker

Conducted clinics for Italian coaches with Hubie Brown, Doug Moe, Dr. Jack Ramsay, and Bill Walton

Conducted clinics for Orlando Magic in China and Japan with Nick Anderson and Penny Hardaway

Other Basketball Involvement

1980–82: Atlanta Hawks scout under Mike Fratello

1997–98: Consultant to Rick Pitino with Boston Celtics

2007–Present: Orlando Magic radio and television color analyst

2009: AAU coach (coached son Adam; team finished season 15-2)

Coaching Wins (Head Coach)

    High School: 148

    College: 142

    NBA: 129

    WNBA: 148

    Women's International: 33

    AAU: 15

    Total: 615